HALF A HUNDRED TALES
of Women

Plus a Collection of Footnotes to History

and a Few Miscellaneous Essays

John Keys O'Doherty

On the Cover

The cover displays a portrait of the author painted in 1978 by Jane Charles of Myrtle Beach, South Carolina. In the years since this example of her early work, Jane has attained widespread recognition as an artist of distinction and importance. Today scores of Charles portraits adorn the halls of public buildings and elegant residences throughout Low Country Carolina.

Illustrations by Ron Carter of Myrtle Beach, South Carolina

Library of Congress Catalog Number: 96-92343
©1996 John Keys O'Doherty
Manufactured in the United States of America on acid-free paper
Printing and composition by Sheriar Press, Myrtle Beach, South Carolina, on 60 lb Benchmark Uncoated Offset
Production Assistant, Monty Martin

Table of Contents

Introduction v
Half a Hundred Tales
    Patriotic Lady Signed the Declaration of Independence 3
    Abigail Adams Called It Home. 6
    Dolley Madison Added Spice to Life in D.C. 8
    Her Memory Endures in Song and Story. 10
    Vivacious First Lady Brought Texas into Union. 13
    Spying System Was Headed by
        Wild Rose of the Confederacy. 16
    The Lady Won Her Fight Against Prejudice 19
    Farm Girl Finds New Life as Young Man 21
    Did a Woman's Whim Influence U.S. History? 24
    Grant's Wife Followed Fashion With Vigor 26
    Woodhull Was a Little Before Her Time 28
    Glamour Girl Is Spy 31
    Lemonade Lucy Respected Traditional Values 33
    No Place for a Lady. 35
    Nellie Bly Abandoned Promising Career. 38
    This First Lady Was National Romantic Idol 41
    Edith Roosevelt — Model First Lady 43
    Belle Grows Up 45
    How Edith Wilson Protected Her Man 47
    Mother Jones Earned a Place in History 49
    Helena: A True Christian 52
    Eccentric Woman Followed a Strange Path 55
    Lady Pursued Unusual Graduate Study 57
    Woman Resurrected as Messiah 59
    Violence Accompanies French Religious Reform 61
    Servant Girl Suffers Persecution. 63
    She Never Knew a Dull Moment 66
    Esther Morris Labored for Justice 68
    Career vs. Motherhood: Is There a Right Answer? 70
    White House Visit Inspires Lofty Dream 72
    She Chose the Life of a Wild West Outlaw 74
    Her Message Carried the Promise of a Better Life 76

She Found that the World Can Indeed Be Cruel 78
The Bread Lady of New Orleans 80
Imagination Built a Fortune 82
This French Heroine Saved Many from Massacre 85
She Climbed a Long, Steep Ladder to
  Professional Distinction 87
She Explored the Horror of Hell on Earth 89
Lady Pirate Dares To Be Different 92
Mountains Will Move 94
She Made Lots of Money with Her Magical Medicine 97
Girl Bandit Goofed Badly 99
"Bluestocking" Lady Found Love 101
This Queen Gave Up Her Throne 103
Circus Actress Assumes Throne 105
She Became Patron Saint of Farm Wives 108
Mercy Missions End in Mysterious Deaths 110
Nameless Waif Attains Notable Niche in History 113

Footnotes to History
  Women in Combat a Matter of Historical Record 119
  A Colony Founded on Greed Perished 121
  How the Puritans Cheated Charles II of Revenge 123
  How Women Won the Right to Vote;
    Adams Ignored Wife's Advice 125
  Modern Feminists Owe Debt to Pioneers 127
  A Blighted Romance Lost an Empire 130
  Casket Girls Created a Unique Culture 132
  An Ally Plotted to Undermine George Washington 134
  Businessman Answers Unique Knock of Opportunity 136
  This Hero Was Rescued from Oblivion 138
  Long Funeral Leads to "Promised Land" 140
  Were These Two Men One and the Same? 142
  They Played a Dangerous Game — and Lost 145
  Pony Express Provided Thrills — for a While 147
  A Little Salt Caused a Lot of Trouble in Texas 149
  Heroic Flyer Earned Small Place in History 151
  Wild West Bandit Defied Lawmen for Years 153
  Luck Ran Out for this Soldier of Fortune 155

Ship Disaster on Mississippi Was Avoidable 157
Big Gun at Naval Academy Memorializes Classic Error 159
Camel Corps Put Strange Beast in Southwest 162
U.S. Subsidized Karl Marx 164
Dickens' Visit to U.S. Stirs Emotional Reactions 167
Newsmen Demonstrate Power of the Press 169
In a Time of Crisis, the President Disappeared 171
U.S. President Banned Christmas Trees. 174

Miscellaneous Essays
   Will 200-Year-Old Prophecy Come True? 179
   Women Seize Political Power 184
   Great Depression Legacy Remains (1979) 187
   Seasonal Signs Point to Romance Ahead 190
   How I Stopped the Show at St. Philomena's 192
   No Lumps, No Burns, No Skin. 195
   Tenderfoot Dream 198
   A Blessing 200
   Christmas Alone 201
Index 203
Bibliography. 207

Introduction

Anyone who hopes to find immortal gems of wisdom or philosophy in these pages is bound to be disappointed. Actually the little book is compiled solely for the entertainment of family and friends of the author as well as any innocent bystanders who may pick up a copy from somebody's coffee table.

The content is comprised of gleanings from the pen of the author over the span of four or five decades, fragments that have appeared in a variety of publications all the way from arctic Alaska to hometown newspapers and sundry periodicals elsewhere. Excluded for obvious reasons are more ponderous materials which for so many years have provided bread and potatoes on the family table.

As the title indicates, the body of the book is divided into sections. First come approximately 50 anecdotes about women in history, the nobility of the species and their more humble sisters, the saintly and the sinful, as well as the lovable and the laughable. All are assembled with admiration and with sympathy as a collective illustration of the wide diversity in the composition of human nature.

Following the ladies comes a section on Footnotes to History consisting of lesser known facts about great events of the past, fragments of information frequently beneath the notice of scholarly architects of academic textbooks.

Lastly, the final pages are devoted to a few miscellaneous essays, also oriented more or less to the past and the vagaries of human nature, always unpredictable and forever beyond all understanding.

Admittedly, this entire project might well be regarded as an exercise in egoism, the last hurrah of a man in the sunset of his years. More importantly, and more emphatically, the book should primarily be regarded as a tribute to the author's spouse of some 65 years. Without her fidelity and perseverence, her painstaking care in safeguarding so many pieces of paper for so many years, this book would never have seen the light of day.

Other friends have contributed substantially to the fodder of encouragement so particularly essential in this case. To all of these a heartfelt message of thanks herewith goes forth. Here is your Book. Enjoy it!!

HALF A HUNDRED TALES OF WOMEN

Patriotic Lady Signed the Declaration of Independence

Not too many Americans are aware that the name of a lady appears on the Declaration of Independence. It is not written in bold script like the signatures of the Founding Fathers. Instead it is inscribed in small, modest letters on the lower right-hand corner. The same lady was also one of the earliest victims of male chauvinist prejudice in the newborn nation of the United States. Here is how it happened.

When Samuel Goddard, a prosperous doctor in colonial America, died in 1762, his son William invested the family inheritance in establishing a newspaper. Unfortunately William was not a very steady fellow. He was interested in everything but could not concentrate on anything for long. After about two years, to save the paper from financial failure, his young sister Mary Katherine took charge of the operation.

An intelligent, energetic girl, she put on the big printer's apron and learned all that had to be known about setting type and feeding paper into the press. She supervised the young apprentices and personally wrote numerous articles for publication. While keeping William with his erratic ideas out of the way as much as possible, she soon had the paper on its financial feet, a highly profitable and respected enterprise. Before too many years passed, the Goddard paper in Baltimore, under management of Mary Katherine, was the most reliable and the most renowned in the colonies.

Forced by circumstances into a career that was not altogether of her choosing, Mary Katherine concentrated on business at an age when other young women were dreaming of courtship and marriage. Because of her dedication she became in time a prominent member of the Baltimore business community. In addition to hard work, two other factors contributed to her success. One was the refreshing informal style of her own compositions in the paper. The other was her fleet of swift horsemen who rushed the news from Baltimore to all the principal communities in the colonies.

In 1775 the Continental Congress ordered Benjamin Franklin

to set up a postal system to serve the needs of the colonies and Franklin promptly appointed Mary Katherine postmistress for Baltimore, an important link in uniting the colonies of the North and the South. His decision was based on her reputation as an outstanding business manager and her experience in distributing her own paper quickly and efficiently. She was the first female to hold an official position under the new provisional government and she served the community well.

The Declaration of Independence was approved by the Continental Congress in July 1776, but not all the distinguished gentlemen had the courage to sign this dangerous document immediately. By the time all signatures were assembled it was January 1777, at which point the Congress was forced to flee from Philadelphia to Baltimore by the approach of British Redcoats. Thus the first authenticated version of the Declaration was ordered printed at Baltimore, and the shop of Mary Goddard was chosen for the job as the best available in the city. Intuitively recognizing the historic significance of the document, Mary printed her full name in the corner as authorized printer instead of the customary initials.

When the war was over, misfortune came into the life of Mary Katherine. Although she had for years managed the printing business as her own, brother William was still the legal owner. Short of cash for some wild scheme, William sold the business, leaving his sister out of any consideration. She continued to serve the city of course as postmistress.

During the years of struggle against the British, there was no provision for salaries for postal officials. The function was performed as a patriotic service. But as the new nation came into being, Congress became a collector and dispenser of money. Before long the office of postmaster became a political plum to be given to friends. One day a young man appeared at the Baltimore post office with a paper saying he was the new postmaster, replacing the incumbent Mary Katherine Goddard.

Baltimore was shocked. Hundreds of citizens signed a petition. Mary herself wrote to President Washington, but it was all to no avail. President Washington checked the problem to the U.S.

Senate, and that august body handed down the opinion that the duties of chief postal officer in Baltimore were too rough for a woman. Mary had then held the office for more than ten years, and the incident can go down in history as an early example of male chauvinist prejudice in the U.S. government.

Mary Katherine died in 1816, an old woman alone and forgotten by the world. In her old age she freed Belinda, the slave girl who attended her, and left Belinda her money. Mary Katherine's name endures on the first authenticated copy of the Declaration of Independence.

Abigail Adams Called It Home

While wars, coronations, assassinations and revolutions are usually emphasized, history is composed as well of the thousand and one small incidents that make up the variety of human nature.

President John Adams and his wife Abigail were the first occupants of the White House when the official mansion was finally completed in 1800 after eight years of stumbling construction. Like any American housewife moving into a new home, the lady Abigail had numerous complaints, many of them directed at the contractor.

Some of the walls in the cold, damp house still were unplastered and the central staircase ended halfway up to the second floor. The President's lady wrote to a friend that the place was habitable only by maintaining fires in 13 fireplaces for 24 hours daily, and wood was hard to find. As for the contractors, wrote Abigail, "promises are all you can get."

Another source of distress for the First Lady was that there was no place to hang the laundry. The open space on the south leading down to Goose Creek was cluttered with shacks and sanitation trenches used by construction workers.

But Abigail Smith Adams was a resourceful woman from a strong New England background. To begin with, she strung her clothes lines in the expanse of the great East Room, although the walls were yet unfinished and unplastered.

Furthermore, in the view of the new White House mistress, the neighborhood was nothing to brag about. With only about 40 real homes scattered about the capital city, the nearest town was the port community of Georgetown about half a mile away. In her correspondence Abigail described Georgetown as "the dirtiest hole I ever saw...a quagmire after every rain."

With characteristic vigor, Abigail Adams pitched in to make only six rooms of the sprawling mansion habitable, leaving the rest for later. After attending to essential living arrangements for her husband and herself, she furnished the upstairs oval room as an appropriate setting for the President to receive visitors.

Because her husband did not win nomination for a second

term, Abigail Adams was mistress of the White House for only four months. Before the Adams family left in March 1801, congressmen, foreign diplomats and the ladies of Georgetown were being entertained weekly in lavish receptions on the upper floor.

When President Thomas Jefferson arrived to succeed John Adams he found the official residence already endowed with an aura of elegance and culture. A remarkable woman of intellect and courage was Abigail Adams. America is indebted to her for a great many accomplishments in a busy and fruitful career.

Dolley Madison Added Spice to Life in D.C.

When President Thomas Jefferson came to the White House in March 1801 he was a widower, but he was nonetheless aware of the important social responsibilities attached to the office of Chief of State. Accordingly, the new President asked the vivacious wife of his Secretary of State, James Madison, to serve as his official hostess.

No selection could have done more to vitalize social life in the capital city. Dolley Madison filled the role superbly. Very soon dignitaries were clamoring for invitations to receptions or dinners at the White House, which became noted not only for the elegance of food and service but also for the brilliance of conversation.

Dinner at the White House was usually served at four in the afternoon with 14 to 20 guests seated without regard to rank around a great circular table.

Dolley's menus included masculine favorites such as wild turkey, mutton and beef pie, as well as a number of feminine delicacies — ice creams copied from the formulas of European masters, feather-light cakes and crepes, all followed by generous servings of excellent wine.

In addition to her role as official White House Hostess, the glamorous Dolley Madison also became the acknowledged leader of Washington social life in general.

When Jefferson's married daughters occasionally came to town for visits, Dolley skillfully guided them about the city to soirees and teas with the very best people.

It was during such a visit that one of the daughters paused long enough to present President Jefferson with a grandson, the first baby born in the White House.

Although Dolley has not been described, even by admirers, as a beautiful woman, she combined all the elegance and polish of fashion with simplicity, frankness and warmth. Dressed elaborately in expensive gowns of latest creation, she had the capacity to put anyone at ease, sometimes by offering a pinch of snuff from the ornate snuffbox she always carried.

Few wives have helped their husband's careers more than did Dolley Madison. When Jefferson's second term as Chief Executive drew to a close, the subject of a successor came up for discussion in the capital city. When the President proposed the name of his good friend and Secretary of State James Madison, there was not a whisper of opposition.

In 1809 Dolley Madison moved into the White House as First Lady in her own right. An appreciative Congress immediately appropriated $30,000 for refurbishing the White House.

The bill provided new chinaware for formal state dinners, $500 for a grand piano, and $1,500 for a new carriage for the President and his lady.

Her Memory Endures in Song and Story

Peggy O'Neale was the daughter of a humble tavern keeper in the capital city of Washington, a witty, vivacious girl with no particular knowledge of politics or statecraft. But because he was kind to Peggy when others were rude, Martin Van Buren became eighth President of the United States.

The story begins in the 1820s when the O'Neale tavern was popular with visitors in search of good beefsteak and beer. General Andrew Jackson and his friend Senator John Henry Eaton were regular patrons who enjoyed the heaping platters distributed by Peggy as she flirted outrageously with the customers. According to rumor, Peggy had a husband in the background, a merchant seaman somewhere far away in the Pacific. If Peggy ever thought of her childish indiscretion, the memory did nothing to dim the sparkle of her Irish personality.

Then in the year 1828 a number of things happened. First, General Jackson was elected President of the United States. Next, news arrived that Peggy's absent husband had been drowned in the China Sea, and Senator John Eaton married the young widow as soon as he decently could. Finally, in a very eventful year, President Jackson announced the appointment of his friend John Eaton to a post in the Cabinet as Secretary of War.

But the long-nosed ladies at the upper levels of Washington society refused to accept Peggy Eaton as an equal. Very quickly in a hundred ways they made it clear that the tavern keeper's daughter was socially unacceptable. The wives of the Vice President and other cabinet members refused to include the Eatons in invitations and snubbed Peggy at every opportunity. Rumors redounded through capital drawing rooms and salons with the unfortunate young bride as the target of venom. All this was very distressing to President Jackson who sadly remembered the hurts inflicted on his own wife in her lifetime by the barbed tongues of busybody women. He asked the members of his cabinet to be less cruel, but they claimed to have no influence over the conduct of their wives. When Jackson's own niece and official White House hostess, Emily Donelson, refused to receive Peggy at the Executive Mansion, an angry President packed her and her husband back to Tennessee.

One cabinet member held himself aloof from this vendetta of social ostracism, Secretary of State Martin Van Buren, a widower and a member of one of the oldest, most honored families in America. On social occasions when they met, Van Buren danced with Peggy as often as possible. He gave elaborate dinners at which the Eatons were guests of honor and made a point of being seen in their company in public places. With all the grace of an old-world gentleman, Van Buren showered Peggy with chivalrous attention. But in spite of it all, poor Peggy and her heartsick husband were forced to endure insult after insult.

President Jackson was equally sick about the business, and finally Van Buren thought of a solution.

If Van Buren were to offer his resignation as Secretary of State, it would then be necessary — in accordance with custom — for all other cabinet members to submit their resignations in turn. The President could then appoint an entirely new cabinet. Reluctantly, after agonizing thought, the President agreed to the plan. And it worked! The great ladies of society saw each of their husbands forced out of high office, and, as it happened, Jackson's new cabinet proved to be a superior group of statesmen. As for the chivalrous Van Buren, he wanted to be ambassador to England, but Jackson instead selected him for Vice President during his second term, while carefully grooming the New Yorker to win the presidency with little effort in the election of 1836. What happened to the glamorous Peggy and the romantic John Henry?

Jackson nominated his friend Eaton as minister to Spain, and at Madrid, the most austerely proper capital in all Europe, Peggy was immediately accepted and became a glorious social success.

The high-toned ladies of Washington condemned Peggy O'Neal not for the sin of being a tavern keeper's daughter, but for being young, and pretty, and charming, and a favorite with all the men who knew her.

A popular song commemorating the charms of Peggy O'Neale can still be heard, particularly in Irish-American communities all across the nation.

Vivacious First Lady Brought Texas into Union

Social life at the White House was pretty dull after President Andrew Jackson retired in 1837, but a few years later the pace picked up considerably when President John Tyler, a middle-aged widower, married a young bride. Julia, the lady of his choice, was big, blonde, beautiful, and about as liberated as a young woman could be in 1844.

Daughter of an old Long Island family, she modeled fashions for fun in New York before her marriage and was a patron of music and the theater.

Although the President had only a year left on his term, the new bride was determined to instill some life into stuffy Washington society. First thing Julia did on arriving at the White House was to hire a press agent, while at the same time setting out to add a touch of zip to formal receptions.

With her love of display the First Lady greeted her guests while seated in a thronelike chair on a raised dais surrounded by twelve white-gowned ladies whom reporters promptly dubbed the Vestal Virgins. Julia's own receiving dress was a purple gown with a long train, set off by a great tiara of ostrich feathers waving above her head.

As for President Tyler, the indulgent husband was delighted with the extensive newspaper coverage attained by his bride. He was particularly pleased when news stories referred to her as the Presidentress, or when her figure and posture were described as Junoesque.

On quiet evenings in the White House, Julia would stand behind her husband's chair, stroking his hair and looking over his shoulder while he worked on official papers. On the following morning the First Lady would judiciously drop morsels of information where they would be most appreciated. Before long, as a result, Julia was recognized as a personage of considerable power.

The year 1844 saw a growing wave of sentiment in favor of

bringing the Republic of Texas into the Union as the 28th state. Julia took up the project as a personal crusade. Using the talents with which nature had so generously blessed her, she called attention to the issue by redoubling her efforts on the social front. First she won the support and admiration of young people by popularizing the polka, considered at the time a wild and shocking dance.

With Julia's help the polka and the waltz became the rage, although President Tyler some years earlier had condemned the waltz as an immoral import from sinful Europe. But the young people of 1844 seized eagerly on the sheet music of the "Julia Waltz" and popularity of the sinful dance flourished.

Even at formal White House dinners her feminine wiles were employed to good purpose. On numerous occasions, in response to a whispered request from Julia, dignified statesmen rose gravely to their feet to propose a toast to Texas. When the lady made such a suggestion to Senator John C. Calhoun of South Carolina, he laughed uproariously and observed with great good humor, "There is no honor in politics."

When the annexation of Texas seemed assured, the First Lady gave her final ball, resolved that Washington would never forget the Tyler administration.

With the help of her enthusiastic press agent, Julia's farewell was designed to go down in history. A thousand candles shed a flood of light over the East Room of the White House, and the younger set in Washington society was present in full force. The hostess wore a gown of white satin embroidered with silver and roses, while three tall ostrich plumes waved from her white satin headdress.

For days after it was over, the newspapers continued to acclaim the party as the most lavish in White House history, and the President was gratified to see numerous references to the First Lady as Juno, this being the name of the queen of the gods in Roman mythology.

Julia Tyler lived another half century after leaving the White House and remained vigorous and attractive through all her years. In her brief tenure as First Lady, Julia gloried in her power and boasted of her influence publicly. Like the younger generation in every age, she was sometimes criticized, but after all, the lady brought Texas into the Union.

Spying System Was Headed by Wild Rose of the Confederacy

The girl who became known as the Wild Rose of the Confederacy grew up in her aunt's Washington boarding house, an old-fashioned 19th Century establishment catering to the appetites of hungry congressmen and senators. A ravishing beauty in her teen-age years, Rose Greenhow counted scores of important government personages among her friends. Growing up was fun for the lively, dark-eyed damsel. Her escorts for social events were glamorous young military officers assigned for duty in the nation's capital.

From among her many suitors, Rose chose a studious young doctor for her husband, but after only a few years of marriage and travel she returned to Washington as a young widow on the eve of the Civil War. Old friends flocked to renew acquaintance, and her house on 16th Street, just a block from the Executive Mansion, became a gathering place for senators, congressmen, cabinet members, and military officers of high and low rank. With her tremendous capacity for attracting men, Rose was easily the most popular hostess in town.

As the nation teetered on the brink of hostilities in 1861, Rose made no secret of her sentiments. After all she had once been a dear friend of the late John C. Calhoun of South Carolina, a brilliant man who took time to explain the doctrine of states' rights to an admiring young girl. From her drawing room in 16th Street, Rose established an intelligence network to serve the Confederacy, using as her weapons the eternally provocative wiles of the female and her knowledge of the vulnerability of men under the blandishments of feminine charm.

Probably the first important act of this bizarre spy system was to warn the Confederate command in Richmond of the impending attack by Federal troops in the summer of 1861. The message was carried by a young girl in a farmer's wagon, with detailed facts and figures sewn into a black scarf tied around her head. A major Confederate victory followed, and emboldened by this success Rose quickly expanded her network of feminine spies until the system included 48 young women in five states. Maps and military information were carried in and out of the city in the concealment of petticoats, corsets, reticules, or whatever other hiding places female ingenuity could devise.

When the famous detective Alan Pinkerton became head of Union secret service, Rose came under suspicion and a watch was placed on her house. The story is told that the great Pinkerton himself, standing in stocking feet on the shoulders of a comrade, maintained nightly vigil at a small window looking into the lady's sitting room. Later he reported witnessing the exchange of documents between Rose and some of her important visitors, but he was unable to assemble concrete evidence.

However, as suspicion continued to grow, Rose was first placed under house arrest and later transferred briefly to the old capital jail.

In spite of all restraint, the spy system was by now so well organized that the flow of information across Union lines to the Confederate command continued unabated. Finally in frustration, the federal government placed Rose and a number of other outspoken Southern ladies on a coastal steamer, ordering the captain to sail south for Confederate territory.

In the Southern capital of Richmond, the Wild Rose of the Confederacy was boisterously received as a heroine, and shortly thereafter she was sent to England on a secret diplomatic mission for the Confederate States. During her stay in London, she put down on paper the full story of her incredible espionage activities, a record still carefully preserved in the National Archives.

Then in September of 1864, bearing a fortune in gold for the Confederate treasury, Rose set sail from England on a ship bound for Wilmington, N.C. As the vessel approached the Carolina coast in the midst of a howling gale, a pair of blockading Yankee gunboats took up pursuit. Bravely the captain made a run for it, but because of the weather the ship was wrecked on a shoal within sight of the friendly Confederate guns at Fort Fisher.

Next day the body of Rose was washed up on the beach, and on the first day of October 1864 a solemn funeral procession made its way through the streets of Wilmington. Tearful soldiers and civilians followed behind the casket draped with Confederate flag, while the guns of Fort Fisher roared defiance to the Yankee gunboats still riding in wait outside the harbor. A monument remains, a great white stone, to preserve the memory of a remarkable woman who combined the use of beauty and brains in dedication to a cause. Here in peace and serenity, the Wild Rose of the Confederacy sleeps forever at rest.

The Lady Won Her Fight Against Prejudice

In the early 1800s few women even thought about becoming doctors since medical colleges in Europe and America simply refused to admit female students. But Miranda Stuart, a determined and energetic young English girl, found a way around this wall of prejudice.

Miranda was the daughter of a wealthy family and might well have lived a life of idle luxury but for a deep-seated ambition to accomplish something. In 1809 she cropped her long hair, donned masculine attire, and applied for admission to the medical college at Edinburgh under the name of James Barry.

Although Edinburgh College was a most prestigious institution at the time, the medical profession was still encumbered by many archaic ideas handed down from medieval times. Training of medical students was primitive and rough. There was no knowledge of asepsis or anesthesia; these discoveries still lay in the future.

Treatment of the sick and injured consisted mostly of administration of harsh purgatives, emetics, and blistering poultices, along with rough and ready surgery. Amputation of the limb was standard treatment for broken bones, and Miranda shared with other students in the grisly task of holding patients forcibly on the table while the instructor demonstrated how to use the surgical saw.

After graduation, Dr. James Barry entered the British army as a medical officer and was sent for duty in South Africa, then a possession of the British Empire. Here the young doctor quickly earned a reputation as an excellent surgeon. As medical inspector for the colony, she placed strict controls on the use of drugs, and was well ahead of her time in applying new ideas of sanitation and hygiene.

As a result of her zeal in cleaning up and modernizing hospitals, jails and leper colonies, she soon found herself stepping on the toes of other colonial officials who resented innovation and progress. Once she was forced to fight a duel and was wounded, but managed to conceal her sex.

Most of all she fought red tape and bureaucratic inertia to improve the treatment of women in hospitals. Jolted out of their lethargy by the doctor's prodding, administrative officials complained about this strutting, bombastic, tyrannical little despot. But her methods were effective.

In 1854 when Great Britain joined in the Crimean War against the Russians, Dr. James Barry was transferred to the battle area. Here, as a surgeon in a field hospital, she had a chance to observe the pioneering work of Florence Nightingale whose dedication to service brought new dignity and respect to the nursing profession.

It has been said that Dr. Barry protected and defended the crusading young nurse when her charges of official inefficiency and indifference were directed against people in high places. As it happened, Dr. Barry before long was in a position to sponsor many of the improvements in hospital services advocated by Florence Nightingale.

Back in England after the war, the doctor moved steadily up the ladder of promotion, while continuing to forge ahead in the introduction of new ideas and new techniques. In due course the energetic little physician became Surgeon General of the British Army, the highest position in the medical service of the greatest army in the world.

Under her leadership, British military medicine laid the foundation for a tradition of scientific research and true professionalism in caring for the sick and wounded.

It was not until Surgeon General Barry died in 1865, at age 70, that her real name and her sex were revealed. Miranda Stuart, petite and slight, demonstrated that a woman could compete successfully in a profession dominated by men. In her remarkable career this talented physician contributed substantially to the advancement of medicine, while encouraging an attitude of compassion and understanding in the treatment of hospital patients.

Farm Girl Finds New Life as Young Man

Sarah Edmonds was born in 1839 on a farm in the Canadian province of New Brunswick. Her father, a cruel and unkind man, was bitter because he had no sons and insisted that Sarah and her younger sister share all the heavy work of the farm, the plowing, the planting, the harvesting, and the eternal back-breaking task of chopping wood.

When Sarah was 17 she borrowed trousers and an old overcoat from a boy living on the next farm. Then on a spring evening, dressed in these old clothes, Sarah slipped away into the woods, in search of a new life across the border in the United States. Leaving Canada and the farm behind, the unhappy girl also abandoned the identity of Sarah Edmonds. Instead a slim young man named Frank Thompson, shabby but bright-eyed and determined, faced a new world looking for work.

Time passed, and in 1861, Frank Thompson, now 22, was living in Flint, Michigan, boarding at the home of the Methodist minister. He was a quiet, smiling young man, well thought-of by everyone in town. He dressed well, and had a good job selling family Bibles from house to house in communities and countryside surrounding Flint. Frank even had his own horse and buggy, something unusual for someone so young.

In his spare time, evenings or weekends, Frank pitched horseshoes or played checkers with other young men in the neighborhood. Occasionally he would invite a young lady, sometimes this one or that, for a walk in the park or a Sunday afternoon drive along the lake.

Then in April 1861 the Civil War broke out. President Lincoln called for 75,000 northern volunteers to fill the ranks of the Union army. Immediately in highly emotional response, virtually all the young men of Flint rushed to the recruiting office. Only Frank Thompson among them all hesitated. What should he do? As his friends and companions took their place in the ranks of the Second Michigan Volunteers, Frank was in danger of being branded a coward by his friends, or even worse, a traitor. But in the hysteria of wartime excitement, there was no time or thought for physical examinations. At last, to the relief of his friends, and only a few days later than most, Frank joined up with the Second Michigan.

The first major battle of the war, at Bull Run, was a major defeat for the North. Frank was assigned as an orderly to help the wounded. Later he served as messenger and postal clerk for his company. Then after two years of the hardships of war, in the spring of 1863, Frank Thompson fell seriously ill. Repeatedly his comrades urged him to seek help at the army hospital, but he refused. Privately he realized his army career must end.

Finally when feeling better, Frank volunteered for undercover duty as a spy. Agents dressed him in old clothes and dyed his skin, his face and all visible parts of his body, with the black pigment used by actors in minstrel shows. Then they sent him through the lines to the South, a clean young black boy who might be hired by the Confederates as a cook or a horse tender.

But the black people Frank met in Carolina were not fooled for a moment by the pigment of his skin. However, with their natural sensitivity the blacks realized that here was a young person in need of help and protection. Frank Thompson disappeared, and the Yankee army listed him as missing in action.

Years later, Frank, or Sarah, revealed what happened. The blacks with their own special ways helped the young person to find a way far to the North, away from the zone of the war. Free at last from her life of deception, Sarah married the boy who years earlier had given her a pair of trousers and an old overcoat. That was in 1867. Three children came along in time to bless the normal ups and downs of marriage. But the strange story of this bizarre military career was not yet over.

When the Second Michigan Volumteers held a 20-year reunion at Flint in 1882, Sarah turned up to join in the celebration, wearing the conventional dress of a respectable middle-aged lady. Fred Thompson's old comrades gave Sarah a tremendous reception.

As a legitimate veteran she was inducted into the Grand Army of the Republic, an organization of Union veterans. In response to an appeal from the Second Michigan, Congress in 1884 awarded

Sarah a pension of $12 a month. When at last she was laid to rest as an old woman under a live oak tree, the limestone marker was inscribed with the legend:

Sarah Edmonds Thompson — Army Nurse.

Did a Woman's Whim Influence U.S. History?

During the spring of 1865, near the closing days of the Civil War, the two most prominent women in Washington detested each other intensely. Each aspired to leadership in the fashionable life of society, although the grand dames of old Georgetown regarded them both with contempt and disdain.

On the one hand was Mary Todd Lincoln, who from the date of her husband's election as President in 1860 expected to be the leading lady of the capital scene.

Instead she found herself mistrusted and disliked. Erratic, temperamental and irritable by nature, Mary Lincoln tried to compensate for her personal inadequacies by tremendous extravagance and repeated displays of imperious arrogance.

She spent money with abandon on satin gowns, jewelry, hundreds of pairs of gloves, and on lavish parties which were criticized as inappropriate for a nation engaged in a tragic war.

In addition, she was extremely jealous, and was particularly suspicious of army officers' wives who were separated temporarily from their husbands by the war. No woman was ever permitted to speak with the President alone.

The opposing role in this comedy of social maneuvering was Julia Grant, easy-going, good-natured wife of General U. S. Grant, commander of all Union armies. Like Mary Lincoln, Julia aspired to social prominence, but with less than complete success. Essentially a plain and unsophisticated person, Julia was impressed by wealth and loved to dress up in satin and lace. Unfortunately, Julia could not distinguish between tasteful elegance and vulgar ostentation. But she knew that Mary Lincoln hated her.

Among other things, Julia could not understand why Mrs. Lincoln expected her women guests to back out of the room when leaving, thus treating her like a royal personage.

On one occasion Julia sat down on a sofa at a Washington party next to Mrs. Lincoln. Quickly, the First Lady moved aside, saying, "How dare you!" This exchange of social slurs was continuous and animated. Historians still speculate on this mutual bitterness as a factor in what happened when at last the war was over.

Following the surrender of General Lee on April 11, General Grant was back in Washington two days later, on the 13th. In the afternoon a note arrived from Mrs. Lincoln inviting him to the White House that evening, but pointedly making no reference to Julia. Grant accordingly declined the invitation. Instead the general and his wife attended a reception at the home of Secretary of War Stanton, who was also at the moment out of favor with the First Lady.

Next day, Good Friday, April 14, a formal invitation arrived from the White House asking the Grants to join the President and the First Lady for a performance that evening at Ford's Theater. But Julia was so angry by this time that, to her husband's dismay, she put her foot down and refused to go.

Instead they pleaded the excuse of an earlier promise to join their children, and after Grant said a personal farewell to the President, they left the city on an afternoon train.

A few hours later, Grant was eating supper in Philadelphia when a telegram arrived to say that Lincoln had been shot in his box at Ford's Theater.

Would Grant's presence at the theater have made any difference? No one knows. The general himself was widely regarded as a likely target for an assassin's bullet. It was well known that President Lincoln was uncomfortable with bodyguards around him, but if Grant had been present the theater would have been thoroughly covered by military security men.

So the incident shows how the strength of a woman's whim can influence the actions of men and perhaps in so doing change the course of history.

Grant's Wife Followed Fashion With Vigor

Not even his best friends would describe Ulysses S. Grant as a great or even a competent President. He rode into office in 1869 on the wave of his record in the Union Army, but as a statesman he proved too weak to lead the country anywhere.

Grant's wife Julia, however, was a lovable person, although a bit cross-eyed. The great sorrow of her life was that the general would never give her the money to have the condition corrected, using the excuse that he liked her as she was.

Following the election of 1868, in which Grant was the victor, Julia decided that the White House was a dingy and inadequate residence. She would much prefer, she told friends, to continue living in her Washington residence a few blocks away.

When this proved to be politically impossible, Julia accepted the inevitable, but proceeded to make some changes in the official mansion. This was the beginning of a time in America when it was fashionable to favor anything that was English or European, particularly anything that was ornate, ornamented, and ostentatious. Following the new fad, Julia laid things on thick.

Gilt, cut glass, heavy chandeliers, and columns sprouted everywhere. Someone said at the time that the rooms looked more like the salons of a steamboat than the residence of the President of a great nation.

The East Room was probably ugliest of all, and it was here the Grants received the 200 guests invited to the wedding of their daughter Nellie in 1874. Nellie, a bright, vivacious, 18-year-old, also brought home something English, the beau she met aboard ship on a cruise to Europe. Invitations placed stress on a "quiet wedding."

Flowers filled the windows, festooned the walls, hung from the chandeliers, and formed arches in the doorways. Under a huge wedding bell of roses, the couple spoke the vows. Nellie's gown, so it was said, contained $4,000 worth of Brussels lace.

Menu for the wedding breakfast, held in the State Dining Room, was printed on white satin (not paper, satin) and featured all the superlatives of the culinary arts. The U.S. Marine Band played faithfully through it all. Gifts for the bride included a $10,000 check from her daddy, a $4,500 dinner service, a $1,000 dinner ring, and a $500 hanky.

With his daughter safely married off, the President went on to spend most of his time at the White House billiard table or at the stables nearby where his beloved horses were kept.

Woodhull Was a Little Before Her Time

The women's lib movement scored a major victory recently (1983) when Sally Rand embarked on a space journey as a fully qualified astronaut. With smug glee, feminist leaders point to this achievement as a major milestone on the pathway to their ultimate goal — presidency of the United States. Is such a thing possible? Many people have forgotten that a woman did in fact run for the presidency a little over a hundred years ago. She didn't win but unquestionably added a touch of spice to an otherwise dull campaign. Her name was Victoria Claflin Woodhull.

During the early 1840's the Claflin family of Ohio could be found wandering over back roads and into small villages in a covered wagon bedecked with tassels and gaudy signs advertising a variety of medications guaranteed to cure every ailment known to man. Strange oriental symbols hinted at secret wisdom handed down from ancient civilizations specializing in study of the universe.

These secret potions were concocted by mom and dad in the back of the wagon, while the two daughters, Victoria and Tennessee, peddled the elixirs from the tailgate. In addition to medicines and cosmetics, the family also dabbled in spiritualism, hypnosis, and magnetism.

As the girls reached teen years, they turned out to be remarkably beautiful, and their charm at the tailgate helped to stimulate sales of the family merchandise. When she was 15, Vickie ran off with a young Doctor Woodhull but soon grew tired of married life and domesticity in a California community. Following her return to Ohio, Vickie and Tennie together made their way to New York where they set up a studio for treatment of disease by magnetism, specializing in stress, emotional fatigue, and other complaints peculiar to big-city businessmen.

Before very long, their clientele included some of the most prominent financial figures in New York, and under the expert guidance of their patrons the girls were soon making money hand over fist in Wall Street. Powerful friends visiting the clinic competed with each other in offering advice and opportunities.

Expanding on this promising start, the girls in due course

opened their own banking house where Vickie and Tennie strutted about with gold pens behind their ears. New York newspapers gave them reams of publicity, referring to the ladies as the Bewitching Brokers and the Queens of Finance. By 1870 things were going so well that Vickie decided to run for President of the United States. Incumbent President Ulysses S. Grant was running for reelection, but he had little to recommend him except for his military record as commander of the Union Army in the Civil War. The Democrats offered Horace Greeley, but the country was not yet ready to restore a Democrat to the White House.

With Tennie as editor, Vickie established her own newspaper to support her candidacy. Her platform was spelled out in detail week after week, including such innovations as equal rights for women, free love, open prostitution, and liberal divorce laws. Quite properly she pointed to her own financial success as an example of what free women could accomplish.

At first Vickie was a sensation. Thousands flocked to hear her speak with a voice of dynamic and commanding vigor. She accepted an invitation to address a Congressional committee in Washington, and the lawmakers rose to give her a standing ovation upon conclusion of her radical speech. Courageous women's groups here and there granted cautious approval, but the organized feminist movement generally was content to sit on the fence awaiting the outcome.

But as election day approached, the forces of prudish self-righteousness and Victorian stuffiness moved in to attack. Rumors were circulated about the standards of Vickie's personal life. Questions were raised about the validity of her divorce from Doctor Woodhull as a young girl. Gossips speculated, probed, and hinted about the propriety of her relationships with patients at the institute for magnetic healing. Barbed tongues cut and slashed at the sisters and their friends.

In retaliation Vickie threatened to expose in her paper the

whole rat's nest of immorality and hypocrisy permeating the upper circles of New York society. And she did! When the lid blew off with a roar the resulting series of scandals and lawsuits clogged the courts of New York for years after. Pillars of the community with secret sins were stripped of the cloak of deceit.

Not surprisingly, Vickie lost the election, but in her own unorthodox way she struck a valiant blow for women's rights. And the story has a happy ending. Both Vickie and Tennie lived to be very old ladies—wealthy and eccentric—and spent their declining years in the quiet respectability of a rose-covered cottage in England.

For further reading: Who's Who in America, 1926-27 (see Victoria Martin); Emanie N. Sachs, "The Terrible Siren" (1928); Leon Oliver, The Great Sensation—Hist. of the Beecher-Tilton-Woodhull Scandal (1873); G. S. Darewin, Synopsis of the Lives of Victoria C. Woodhull and Tennessee Claflin (London, 1891); M. F. Darwin, One Moral Standard for All; Extracts from the Lives of Victoria Woodhull . . . and Tennessee Claflin (1895); Madeleine Legge, Two Noble Women (1893); Henry Clews, Fifty Years in Wall Street (1908); records of Tilton-Beecher trial, City Court, Brooklyn, Jan.-June 1875; H. G. Clark, The Thunderbolt (1873); Theodore Tilton, Golden Age Tracts, No. 3, (Victoria C. Woodhull (1871); obituary of Tennessee Claflin in N.Y. Times, Jan. 20, 1923; obituary of Victoria Woodhull, Ibid., June 11, 1927. American Heritage, June 1956 . Volume VII, Number 4., p. 44-47.

Glamour Girl Is Spy

Peggy Cashman was a lovely dark-eyed beauty who spent her best years fighting off the amorous advances of men. She was born in New Orleans in 1833, but a few years later her parents moved to Michigan to set up a trading business with the Indians. As she grew up to teen-age, according to Peggy's own account, she was forced to deal with numerous improper proposals from frontier roughnecks, and in doing so she gained quite a reputation for her skill with a horsewhip.

Thoroughly bored nevertheless with her frontier existence, Peggy left home at 18 to become an actress. She found work with a traveling company, playing secondary parts in melodramas for small-town audiences. The fateful magnetism by which she attracted men grew more intense, but Peggy spurned all romantic approaches, proper and improper alike.

While touring the South during the War Between the States in 1863, Peggy fell under he spell of an older man who treated her with fatherly affection. He confided that he was a spy for the North and would pay well for her help in obtaining military information to be sent across the lines to Yankee forces. Peggy agreed to help.

By lavishing her provocative smiles on romantic young Confederate officers she soon wheedled small snips of information from them. However in no case did these romantic encounters advance beyond a quick squeeze of the hand or a chaste kiss on the cheek. Inevitably someone became suspicious of the beautiful tease who dealt in false promises, who flirted without warmth and kissed without feeling.

One evening after finishing her performance at the theater Peggy was returning to her hotel when her coach was stopped by a Confederate patrol. Ignoring her protests, the officers in charge searched Peggy with more diligence than a lady would normally expect. Sure enough, concealed artfully in her clothing were the damning evidences of her treachery, drawings of fortifications, names of regiments, schedules of troop movements. Without further ceremony the lady was placed behind bars under guard.

Her trial by military court was prompt and brief, but all the rules were carefully observed. In accordance with military law, Peggy was sentenced to be shot as a spy. But before the sentence could be carried out, a roving patrol of Yankee cavalry descended by night on the jail and carried her across the lines to safety.

Returning to the theater after her narrow escape from death, Peggy found that her fame as a spy was a great help in her career. She was given better parts and her name was printed in prominent letters. Unfortunately her acting was not really very good, and Peggy was sharp enough to see that her role as a star would not last for long.

Accordingly, at the close of a performance in Casa Grande, Arizona, the lady announced from the stage that she had accepted a proposal of marriage, thus bringing an end to her theatrical career and her lifelong rejection of men. At that time Peggy was 43 years old.

Perhaps because the bloom of youth was past, or because the element of true love was lacking, the marriage was not a success. Three days after the wedding the groom ran away with the plump little Mexican girl who worked as maid at the hotel. First thought of the deserted bride was to return to her professional career in the theater, but no suitable parts could be found for her. She sent messages to old friends in the business, but no answers came in reply to her letters and telegrams. To tide her over the crisis, Peggy accepted a position as hostess and receptionist at the town saloon. Even this did not last. Somehow the magic that had once attracted men like moths to a flame had mysteriously flickered away.

From this point forward, life grew progressively more unkind to Peggy. She drifted west with the great tide of population, doing whatever work she could find to support herself. Each new job was a little more demeaning than the last. In San Francisco for a time she worked as a domestic servant, but the sight of other women living in love and harmony with husband and children was more than Peggy could bear. In the loneliness of solitary nights she reflected sadly on opportunities missed and the lost dream of life as it might have been.

Only when she died was her name once more briefly remembered. A group of Union war veterans, recalling her moment of drama as a Yankee spy, raised the money to have her laid to rest with respectable decency.

Lemonade Lucy Respected Traditional Values

When Rutherford B. Hayes became 19th President of the United States in 1877, the country was pretty much tired of the corruption, vulgarity and excesses of the administration that had gone before.

A quiet and religious family from Ohio, the Hayes, with their seven children, presented a welcome return to traditional values in the eyes of most Americans.

Shortly after arriving at the White House, Lucy Hayes issued an order to the staff forbidding service of any wines or spirits at functions in the presidential mansion. Her decision was based less on any Puritanical prejudice than on the need to restore proper respectability to the home of the first family.

Members of the diplomatic corps and other Washingtonians, long accustomed to the use of alcohol as a relish with their meals, were dismayed at the prospect of sitting through long official affairs without stimulant.

Around town before long the President's wife became known as lemonade Lucy. One congressman was heard to complain loudly about a presidential dinner that was "washed down with coffee and cold water."

Before long, and unknown to the President or his wife, a White House steward was bribed on occasion by thirsty guests to add a bit of rum to the Roman punch, a concoction of sherbert, lemon juice and egg white which was served at the middle of the meal as a refresher. Among the initiated, the Roman punch course became known as the "Life-Saving Station." The President and his wife never knew.

Life at the White House during the Hayes administration was simple and wholesome. Every morning the President led the family in prayer before breakfast, and most evenings were spent in the intimacy of the family circle, sometimes with Secretary of the Interior Carl Schurz entertaining at the piano while the children sang their favorite songs. Mrs. Hayes, incidentally, initiated the custom of Easter egg rolling on the White House lawn each year.

Lucy Hayes was the first wife of an American president to have attended college. While this family was in residence, the first telephones were installed in the White House, but the newfangled technology made little difference in the habits of an old-fashioned American family.

No great monumental changes took place during those years, but to his credit let it be noted that the administration of Rutherford B. Hayes marked the beginning of the end for Reconstruction in the South.

No Place for a Lady

American journalism in its earliest years was a product of the spirit of rebellion, an incitement to revolution, and perhaps understandably the voice of dissent against tyranny was dominated by masculinity.

But for all the lusty boisterousness of the profession in its infancy, a few women managed to gain entrance into the ranks of those who by the power of the pen shaped attitudes and popular opinion for the nation.

First woman journalist in the history of the American colonies was Elizabeth Timothy of Charles Town who published the South Carolina Gazette in 1738. A few years later when Andrew Bradford died in Philadelphia, his wife continued publication of the *American Weekly Mercury*. Then there was Catherine Zenger, an active publisher in New York, Ann Franklin in Rhode Island, and Clementina Rind in Richmond.

All these women were widows of printers in an age when the printshop was a family business and the wife and children simply carried on after loss of the husband and father.

In those early years of personal journalism, reporters were not necessary. Columns were filled with official documents, letters, shipping lists, and the individual opinions of editors.

This began to change after about 1840 when newspapers assumed a more extensive scope, with greater emphasis on local news and utilizing a greater variety of talent.

However, middle-class America by this time regarded journalism, like the music hall stage, as a profession unsuitable for respectable young ladies. For this reason, pioneer newswomen avoided the spotlight and made use of pseudonyms or pen names.

The first Washington gossip column was written by Anne Royal under the name of Paul Pry. Later she labeled her column simply *The Huntress*, a title with a somewhat frightening predatory connotation.

When Lizzie Kelly of Pittsburgh was offered a job on the local paper, her two brothers insisted that she use a false name to protect the family honor and insisted too that her mother accompany the girl when she delivered her stories to the editor's office. Lizzie in print became Nellie Bly, the name borrowed from a popular song, and Nellie went on to become the nation's first investigative reporter, striking terror into the hearts of corrupt politicians.

To Horace Greeley of New York, energetic and erratic giant of the newspaper world, must go credit for bringing the first true woman intellectual into American journalism. The lady was Margaret Fuller, a brilliant mind, feminist, philosopher, and friend of Ralph Waldo Emerson, the Sage of Concord.

For a time she was editor of a literary magazine *The Dial*, known as the voice of New England transcendentalism. Greeley, who had the odd idea that journalism had no place for college men, hired her as his assistant.

He sent her to Europe to cover the fighting in Italy during the revolution of 1848, and few writers of either sex have since matched the emotional impact of her work as a war correspondent.

On the way home to New York in 1850 the ship bearing Margaret along with her Italian husband and infant baby was wrecked in a storm within sight of Long Island. Two days later the dead infant was washed up on shore, but the body of Margaret was never recovered.

The most important of early women's magazines in America was Godey's *Lady's Book* founded in 1830 at Philadelphia. Sarah Josepha Hale, author of the nursery rhyme *Mary Had a Little Lamb*, became editor in 1836.

Over the years Godey's became famous for hand-colored illustrations of pretty ladies with their beruffled hoopskirts and equally pretty gentlemen with tapered trousers and narrow waists.

A few years later, a woman using the name Ann S. Stephens became editor of a rival publication, *Peterson's Magazine*. In addition to her other duties, editor Ann wrote romantic love serials that ran interminably for uncountable months — forerunner of modern soap operas.

At the beginning of the 20th century America had an inferiority complex about native talent in the literary arts. Nothing could conceivably have genuine artistic merit unless it originated in the Old World.

Scores of American poets and writers flocked to Europe in search of recognition. Among these were Robert Frost, T. S. Eliot, Ezra Pound, Amy Lowell, to name just a few.

In 1912 in Chicago a middle-aged woman named Harriet Monroe decided that this whole sense of inferiority was ridiculous. So, with money wheedled in driplets from friends, Harriet Monroe founded a new publication, *Poetry, a Magazine of Verse,* to provide a voice for American poets in their own country.

Today, 66 years later, the little magazine survives, not as a money-making enterprise, but as eloquent evidence of the distinctive artistic quality of American poetry.

There are others to be sure who might be mentioned, ladies who cut their literary teeth on newspaper assignments and then went on to artistic greatness. Among these were Fanny Hurst, Faith Baldwin, Dorothy Parker and Dorothy Thompson.

Nellie Bly Abandoned Promising Career

This is the story of Nellie Bly, girl newspaper reporter, whose name once struck fear in the hearts of corrupt politicians and crooked public officials. As a pioneer in the field of investigative reporting, Nellie blazed a trail for others to follow and proved that a virtuous young girl with talent could win success in the big city.

It all began nearly 100 years ago when Lizzie Kelly, a teenage girl in Pittsburgh, wrote a letter to the editor of the local paper scolding him for something he had said. So impressed was the great man by Lizzie's eloquence and sincerity that he invited her to write some more observations for his paper, for a small token payment.

Lizzie was thrilled, but her mother and two brothers were outraged by the insult. In the year 1880 such an offer to a young girl amounted virtually to an indecent proposition. No respectable woman would permit herself to be seen near a newspaper office where rough men chewed tobacco and cursed each other in foul language. Furthermore, no nice girl would permit her name to be printed in a newspaper.

But Lizzie wept and pleaded. Her life would be ruined if her ambition were so cruelly stifled.

Finally the brothers agreed that to avoid family disgrace, Lizzie would use a false name. She would write her stories at home, locked in her room, and her mother would walk with her to deliver them to the editor, preferably at dusk when no one would recognize them. So began the career of Nellie Bly, girl journalist, the name being borrowed from a popular song of the day.

After a year of this secret career, Nellie decided she was ready for the big time, New York City with its many newspapers and numerous glamorous personalities. There was little opposition at home. Nellie's mother, always uneasy about the family reputation, felt that if a girl had to be a newspaper person it was better to do it somewhere else far away. Nellie naturally wrote ahead to New York for lodging at a respectable boarding house, and the kindly landlady met her at the railroad station to escort her safely through city streets.

The next few weeks were discouraging as Nellie knocked vainly at door after door. Finally she persuaded an editor to try one of the innovative ideas clamoring for expression in her youthful head.

Here was the plan: Nellie would proceed to some public place and pretend to be insane, not violently dangerous, but moderately demented. Inevitably she would be consigned to the city mental hospital on Bedloe's Island. Then after a few days or so, the paper would reveal her real identity, and Nellie would be released to write an account of her experience. The editor went along to the extent of putting her on the payroll as a temporary worker.

Sure enough, after a few days of examinations and questioning, Nellie found herself committed by a judge to Bedloe's Island. An excellent actress, she had deceived all the doctors.

But, unknown to Nellie, on the day she entered the institution, the editor who had hired her died suddenly at his desk. A heart attack, people said. As days passed, Nellie found that she had more time for investigation than she had bargained for. Finally somebody at the newspaper remembered her. Nellie's story, written from the heart, was a sensation. Nellie Bly was on her way to fame.

For her next assignment, Nellie picked a man's pocket in Times Square. Her story on the workings of municipal court and conditions in the city jail was featured under banner headlines. Then she went to the state capital at Albany and bribed a legislator to vote against a particular bill. Back at her desk in the city, she exposed him.

From then on life was one great adventure after another. Nellie became adept in the use of costume and disguise, sometimes adopting the role of an old grandmother, a vulgar woman of the slums, or even a lady in the spicy world of New York after dark. Every story was a winner. Publications all over the country were offering top prices for Nellie's work.

Suddenly when the young girl reporter was at the pinnacle of her career, the name Nellie Bly disappeared completely from sight. Vainly did readers turn the pages in search of her appetizing literary fare. All New York and much of America wondered what had happened.

To understand the mystery of her disappearance it is necessary to remember that Nellie Bly was really two persons in one. On the surface was the star reporter, the career woman fighting the world with her trusty pen. Underneath was the personality of Lizzie Kelly, a wholesome young American girl from Pennsylvania.

Thus when Bob Waterman, owner of a small factory in Brooklyn, proposed marriage, Nellie Bly hesitated in her decision, but Lizzie Kelly said yes.

When she left the newspaper office for the last time, Nellie stood on the steps looking out at the milling throngs of people on the street. Then placing her hand on the arm of her sweetheart, she ended her career with the simple words: "Fame is fleeting, but love is forever."

This First Lady Was National Romantic Idol

Feminine hearts fluttered all over Washington when President Grover Cleveland moved into the White House in 1885.

A handsome mustachioed New Yorker with courtly manners, the new President was clearly the nation's most eligible bachelor. Here and there a few busy tongues whispered of romantic attachments earlier in the big man's life, but the new President's secret true love was a young college student named Frances Folsom, daughter of a former law partner.

Being a thorough gentleman, Cleveland held his silence until Frances had completed her studies at Wells College in upper New York state. When he finally proposed, and she shyly accepted, the President was 50 and the bride-to-be was 22.

Washington society grew wild with excitement over the prospect of a White House wedding, but the President invited only close friends and members of his cabinet. The invitations, written in Cleveland's own hand, mentioned a "very quiet affair" for Wednesday evening at seven.

Actually the quiet affair turned out to be something else entirely. When the bride, slim, dark-haired and incredibly lovely in a gown of white satin took her place in the Blue Room, the spoken ceremony was simple enough.

But as guests arrived at the portico they were greeted by John Philip Sousa conducting the Marine Band in scarlet and gold uniforms. Garlands of roses lighted by flickering candles decorated the halls leading from the entrance.

When the groom bent to kiss the bride, church bells rang out all over the city and a 21-gun salute was fired from the Washington Navy Yard. Crowds of citizens gathered on the White House lawn to cheer themselves hoarse.

Young, beautiful, and completely gracious, the new First Lady became the greatest vitalizing force in Washington social life since the days of Dolley Madison half a century earlier. White House receptions were thronged as never before.

Frances Cleveland became America's symbol of romance, and people from all over the country flocked to Washington just to shake her hand in a reception line and report back home on the radiance of her smile. More than once the young First Lady received medical treatment for fingers bruised by eager admirers.

For three years the bride of the 22d President was a sparkling hostess for the nation during one of the most active periods in the social life of the nation's capital.

When Cleveland's term ended in March 1889, Frances said goodbye to the White House staff, and asked them to guard all her little treasures, vowing that she would some day return. Sure enough, four years later the Clevelands returned to the White House when the handsome New Yorker was elected for another term.

Grover Cleveland was the only President to be married in the White House and the only President to serve two terms which were not consecutive. When Frances and her husband came back to Washington in 1893, the Clevelands were then proud parents of two baby girls.

Edith Roosevelt — Model First Lady

When Edith Roosevelt became the nation's First Lady in September 1901, she proved to be the most efficient family manager ever to occupy the White House.

With six children ranging from teen-agers to toddler — and a husband who in some ways never grew up — she was the calm center of an uproarious storm of activity that endured for more than seven years.

The children of President Theodore Roosevelt were born at an old-fashioned country house on Long Island, and when the family moved to Washington they brought along an abundance of natural energy and exuberance.

On rainy days the carpeted stairs of the Executive Mansion became a ski slope, with the help of huge metal serving trays borrowed from the kitchen. Halls reverberated to the sound of roller skates, and potted palms were great for hide-and-seek.

Seventeen-year-old Alice loved to startle strangers on dress-up occasions by producing a pet snake from her purse. Pets were part of the family, including dogs, flying squirrels, kangaroo rats and a badger.

A favorite member of the menagerie was a pony which the children smuggled into the house and upstairs to visit a sick brother one evening.

Following bedtime-storybook sessions in the family quarters, pillow fights were frequent, with the President himself participating when official duties permitted.

While the President was laying the foundations for the United States as a world power and planning the Panama Canal, Edith exercised benevolent control over the family bedlam and performed the official functions of

First Lady with poise and charm. She was first to employ a social secretary but supervised the operation of the household personally, giving daily instructions to maids and kitchen workers. Guest lists were carefully selected on the basis of personalities and compatibility, so that official dinners were always a sparkling success.

White House living space at the time was wholly inadequate for such a large family. Children in bathrobes and slippers frequently encountered clerks or messengers in the halls.

Using her powers of persuasion on the President, Edith initiated a major program of renovation. Improvements included installation of modern plumbing and private baths, extensive use of electricity, and provision for central heating.

When the work was finished, the Roosevelts formally designated the official residence as the White House, a term that had been used only occasionally and informally up to that time.

Edith Roosevelt and her family left the White House after serving more than seven years. As the family departed, a member of the staff paid an eloquent tribute to the performance of a great First Lady. "In all that time, she never made a mistake."

Belle Grows Up

Her name was Juliette, and the story of her early years reads like a chapter from a romantic fairy tale. She was born in 1860 at Savannah, in a great sprawling mansion with rolling lawns, luxuriant flower gardens, and lots of servants. Because she was a delicate child, fragile as a spring flower it was said, the servants called her Daisy, and the nickname endured through all the years of her life.

When Daisy was four in 1865, news came that General Sherman's army was approaching from the west, intent on burning the city. As the sound of big guns grew closer, Daisy and her mother escaped by boat and eventually made their way to Chicago where Grandfather Kinzie was government agent for Indian affairs. Here the bright-eyed Daisy found new sources of childhood delight, playing with Indian boys and girls, making dolls from twigs, and watching the Indian women as they went about the domestic chores of the camp.

Back in Georgia after the war, Daisy's life as a wealthy young Southern belle moved from one pinnacle to the next. In her teens she was an excellent swimmer and rider, a popular dancer, while showing evidence of talent in the arts. Finishing school at an exclusive academy for young ladies added the ultimate polish in the social graces.

Then at a ball in Savannah, Daisy met a handsome, aristocratic young Englishman visiting the New World to study the cultivation of cotton. Their engagement was announced soon after.

At the wedding, the most elaborate of the season, an extraordinary accident occurred. Unknown to the bride at the time, as the happy pair ran through a shower of rice, a single grain lodged in her ear, causing Daisy to become deaf in her later years.

After her marriage, life for Daisy was even more like a story-book fantasy. Making their home in England, the young couple became active in fashionable upperclass social life. Daisy was presented at the court of Queen Victoria, and many of the famous personages of the day were her friends and associates. An occasional transatlantic visit to Savannah punctuated the happy years of romantic delight.

Suddenly one day the fairy tale ended. In dismay Daisy watched her beloved William sicken and die under onslaught of a quick, incurable illness. Desolation engulfed her as everything in her world turned overnight into ashes.

For a period of years to follow Daisy traveled from city to city and from country to country like a lost soul in search of something unknown. Her friends tried to comfort her, to restore her interest in life, but their words held no cheer. Like a person sentenced to banishment from the past, she wandered, homeless and alone, in search of a future. She became obsessed with the conviction that her life was a waste. Everything that once she had treasured had been stolen from her, leaving an emptiness that could not be filled.

After some years spent in this prison of her mind, Daisy one day came home to Savannah. Miraculously it seemed, her zest for life had returned, and the sparkle in her eyes was restored. With eager enthusiasm she spoke of an idea, an idea she felt sure would give purpose and meaning to all her remaining years.

As a first step, Daisy invited eight young girls to a tea at her old family home in Savannah. When everyone was comfortably seated she spoke to them of what was on her mind. And as she talked her guests responded enthusiastically to her idea. It was an idea destined to enrich the lives and strengthen the character of millions of American girls for years and years to come.

Daisy's full name was Juliette Gordon Lowe. She presided over the very first meeting of the Girl Scouts of America at a tea party in Savannah on March 12, 1912.

How Edith Wilson Protected Her Man

In the summer of 1915 President Woodrow Wilson was still in mourning for the death of his first wife when he met an attractive dark-eyed widow from Virginia. Actually the meeting was accidental.

Edith Bolling Galt went to the White House that afternoon to have tea with a friend on the presidential staff. When Wilson returned unexpectedly early from a golf game, he joined the women and was immediately smitten.

From that meeting on, Edith Galt was a frequent guest at the Executive Mansion. Sixty days later the President proposed on the South Portico overlooking the broad sweep of lawn leading down toward the river.

They were married quietly a week before Christmas at the home of the bride a few blocks away. So began for Edith Wilson an experience such as no First Lady has lived through before or since.

Little did she know that she would be called upon to run the government of the United States for a year and a half.

Tragedy struck the Wilsons when the President collapsed from exhaustion while on a speaking trip to the West. Two weeks later at the White House a severe stroke paralyzed his left side leaving him speechless and wholly incapacitated. Only Mrs. Wilson and the White House physician were aware of the extent of the President's illness, and resolutely she set out to protect her husband from the world.

White House gates were locked to keep out visitors and all appointments were immediately canceled. With no political experience and only two years of formal schooling, Edith Wilson took over the job of running the government. All memoranda, petitions, diplomatic documents, and Congressional mail addressed to the President were received and examined by the First Lady.

Most of the material she discarded immediately into the trash, and devoted her attention only to those items she felt to be important. Outgoing mail the next day was signed with an indecipherable scrawl purporting to be that of the President. Routine letters were signed candidly with the name of the First Lady.

Each afternoon at four, the First Lady received members of the cabinet in her sitting room where they presented information on national affairs.

This information, she dutifully promised, would be passed on to the President for his evaluation and a decision to be relayed at tomorrow's meeting. These decisions were sometimes verbal and sometimes typed over the illegible scrawled signature.

With the passage of time the President showed some slight improvement, and in due course a few close friends were permitted to see him. His career, of course, was at an end.

In March 1921 the Wilsons left the White House, ending one of the strangest and potentially most dangerous episodes in American history.

Edith Wilson took neither pride nor satisfaction in her remarkable accomplishment in running the affairs of the United States for months alone. By her own account, it was done to save her husband, so that he might use the little strength he had to throw off his illness.

Mother Jones Earned a Place in History

Mary Harris Jones lived to be more than a hundred years old. In the first half of her long life she learned in full measure the meaning of heartbreak and tragedy. But in the second 50 years she became known as the militant female Mother Jones, one of the most remarkable figures of her time, as she fought to end the cruelties of child labor in American mills and factories.

About 1835 the Harris family from Ireland came out to Chicago in search of a better existence. Young Mary grew up to be a school teacher and accepted a job in Memphis where she married an iron worker named Jones in 1861. Six years later an epidemic of yellow fever swept the city. Rich people fled from the plague, but hundreds of those who were left died, virtually overnight.

One by one Mary's four children caught the dread disease and coughed out the last breath of life in her arms. She washed each small body in turn and placed it on the front step to be picked up by the death wagon sent out each day by sanitation authorities on a grisly round of collection. Finally Mary's husband collapsed in fever and died within hours.

With no ties to keep her in Memphis, Mary returned to Chicago where she opened a dress shop on a street near the lake. For a short time things went well. Then in October 1871, the great Chicago fire burned most of the city leaving thousands of people homeless. During that terrible night, Mary and her neighbors were forced to wade out into the lake to escape ferocious heat and falling embers.

Once more homeless and destitute, Mary Jones found refuge in an old scorched shed used by the Knights of Labor, the first organization of working men in America. From these men Mary learned about early efforts of workers to improve conditions of employment and wages through unified actions.

Very soon the little woman with the high falsetto voice became a militant activist with the Knights of Labor in the battle to end exploitation of workers. She became known as Mother Jones and was particularly interested in exposing the abuses of child labor in mills and factories, as well as in the coal fields where young boys worked in underground tunnels too small to admit men.

Listeners were spellbound by her dramatic description of the mistreatment of young workers. Invariably she carried an umbrella, in fair weather or foul, which she brandished overhead like the upraised sword of an avenging angel. She scoured the mills of New England to observe conditions of child labor, and the speeches which followed were inflammatory and sometimes profane.

A favorite dramatic gesture at her meetings was to hold aloft the mutilated hand of a youngster injured by machinery and shout the question: "What is the price of fingers in the New England textile market today?"

In 1899 Mother Jones organized a march of factory children from Philadelphia to New York to call attention to the 14-hour day at wages as low as 10 cents an hour.

For the children the march was a great adventure, an extended summer picnic offering more freedom than they had ever known. They took along tin plates and cups as well as a big wash boiler to cook their food by the roadside. Along the line of march, farmers showered the children with fresh fruits and vegetables. Wives came down to the road with extra clothing and homemade pies or cakes. The children slept in barns or community meeting halls. In some small towns the police were unfriendly but the spirit of the marchers was not dampened.

Despite her own independent ways and her strong sense of justice, Mother Jones never cared about the right to vote for women. When a group of ladies at a New York dinner hailed her as the new champion of feminism, she shocked them with her outspoken observations.

Most of the women present, she stated, were caught up in the suffragist movement because it was novel and fashionable. Women's liberation was more a subject of drawing room conversation than a social or political movement.

Even 40 years after the death of her family in Memphis, Mother Jones continued to wear mourning, a long widow's dress of severest black. To compensate for her small stature she wore a tremendous hat, also jet black, and the whole costume gave her a fearsome supernatural appearance. On her one hundredth birthday,

May Day 1930, she posed for newsreel cameras. When asked if she still grieved for her children, she answered that her motto was "Pray for the dead, but fight for the living." A few weeks later she died of old age.

Helena: A True Christian

The Easter season is an appropriate time to honor the memory of a great Christian lady named Helena, a devout believer who used the power and privilege of her royal position to further the cause of Christianity throughout the known world.

Do you remember the childhood nursery rhyme about Old King Cole, the Merry Old Soul? Old King Cole was a real person who reigned over a section of England in A.D. 250 when the Romans dominated the entire world. When the Roman emperor Chlorus visited England, he was enchanted by the beauty of King Cole's daughter Helena and took the girl back to Rome as his bride.

Both King Cole and his daughter had earlier been converted to the new Christian faith, and Helena was grieved to see how Christians were persecuted and oppressed in the Roman capital. As wife of the emperor, she was obliged to visit the public games frequently, where seated in the royal box she saw Christian martyrs thrown to wild beasts or put to death under the swords of gladiators.

When Helena gave birth to a son, Constantine, she brought him up as a Christian, teaching him the new faith in the privacy of her apartment. This secret she kept carefully from her husband because of his hatred for followers of the Nazarene.

After Helena and Chlorus had been married for nearly 20 years, the emperor cast her aside in pagan fashion in favor of a younger woman. No one would risk the emperor's wrath by helping her, and Helena was left destitute and homeless to make her own way in the world.

Time passed and presently Chlorus died. His son Constantine ascended the throne, the first Christian emperor in the long history of Rome. Immediately, the new ruler instituted a great search for his lost mother, and having found her, Constantine restored Helena to a position of honor in the royal household.

Under influence of the pious Helena, Constantine became a great champion and supporter of the Christian faith. When the emperor ordered construction of a magnificent church at the site of the crucifixion on Mount Calvary, the empress-mother journeyed to Jerusalem to superintend the work in person.

While in the Holy Land, Helena found the place where she believed the tomb of Jesus to have been, but a temple to the pagan goddess Venus had been erected on the spot. Helena ordered the pagan temple destroyed, and directed her workmen to search for the sacred cave where the body of Jesus lay for three days. Nearby, adjacent to the garden of Joseph of Arimathea, Helena also found what she believed to be the true cross upon which Jesus was crucified.

In the area where the cross of Calvary and the tomb were found, Helena built the Church of the Holy Sepulchre, and this church still stands amid the cluster of buildings that have since been added over the centuries. The heart of this great church is the chapel of the Holy Sepulchre, and the feet of generations of pilgrims have worn smooth the steps leading to the spot where Helena found the cross.

Next, this devout lady built the Church of the Nativity at Bethlehem above a hillside grotto believed to be the site of the manger. In no other church have so many Christians worshipped for so many centuries.

Although she was now an old lady, Helena remained in the Holy Land, assisting individuals and entire communities by her good works. In true Christian fashion she cared for the poor and devoted many hours to instructing young people in the doctrines of the Christian faith.

When Helena died in A.D. 330, her son Constantine and his children were at her bedside. The emperor then ordered that his mother be buried with the utmost honor and ceremony. Special coins were minted to mark her passing and were distributed to the farthest corners of the Roman Empire. Following a massive funeral ceremony, the body of Helena was transported to Byzantium, or Constantinople, where the emperor had built a magnificent new capital.

Here in Constantinople the embossed coffin was placed in the imperial vault at the Church of the Apostles, adjacent to the tomb the emperor had reserved for himself.

A devoted mother and a devout Christian, Helena continues to be revered for her piety and her multitudinous good works. An important point to remember is that it was the Emperor Constantine, son of Helena, who recognized and legalized the Christian church in the Roman Empire after 300 years of persecution and oppression.

Eccentric Woman Followed a Strange Path

Margery Kempe died in England about 1438, more than half a century before Columbus discovered America, and the world quickly forgot her.

About five hundred years later, in 1934, an American professor puttering around an old English library stumbled on a document that had been overlooked for years in a corner. This old paper, dry and yellowed with age, contained the life story of a woman, a vain and intensely passionate woman who in her later years was regarded as an eccentric. Margery Kempe was the first woman to write her autobiography in the English language, and she was mercilessly honest in recording the details of her character and the unusual events of her life.

Accordingly to Margery's own story, she was born in 1373, the only daughter of the mayor at the village of Lynn. As a young girl she loved fine clothes and enjoyed parading about the village streets to attract the admiring glances of men. At times she loitered near the mill, and near the tavern, places where men were likely to congregate.

Margery was barely into her teens when she became the bride of a prominent citizen who owned both the mill and the brewery. In the busy years that followed she presented her husband with 14 children as rapidly as nature would permit. Following the birth of the 14th, the couple appeared before the local bishop and swore a reverse marriage oath, meaning that they would henceforth occupy separate beds and refrain from the sin of the flesh. From this point forward Margery turned her attention to affairs of the spirit, devoting much of her time to prayer and intensive meditation.

Like Joan of Arc, Margery soon began to hear mysterious voices in the air, and like some of the early Christians, she presently acquired the ability to heal. Once when a woman lost her mind in the agony of childbirth, Margery told her that angels were hovering in the room and all would soon be well.

On another occasion when the village church caught fire,

Margery entered the building and knelt to pray. Although sparks were falling about her, she remained in place until men with snow on their shoulders entered to tell her that Providence had sent a snowstorm to quench the fire.

Some time later, Margery set out alone to visit the Holy Land. Never in her tale does she mention any problems with money, so presumably both the mill and the tavern continued to prosper. In those days travel was dangerous, particularly for women, but the adventurous lady ignored all warning of peril to her life or her person. When she was stranded in Italy, she promptly bought ship passage from a pirate captain whose vessel delivered her safely to her destination. As a pilgrim in Jerusalem, Margery then set out to tour the historic shrines of Christianity mounted on the back of a small donkey.

On returning to her native England, Margery was filled with renewed religious fervor. She became an itinerant preacher, wandering from town to village and wherever an audience could be found. In appearance she looked rather like an Old Testament prophet, dressed in a single garment of canvas and with unkempt hair falling to her waist. Margery's story does not reveal her own personal ideas about salvation, but regular churchmen of the time did not approve of her. Many pastors would not permit her to enter the doors of their churches. Even in her native village of Lynn, jeering children followed her in the street, and because of her eccentric ways she was once stoned as a witch.

As the years at last took their toll, Margery quietly settled down in the privacy of a small cottage to write her book. It was no easy task. Virtually all books at the time were written in Latin. Paper and ink were commodities not readily available in a country village. The local priest offered to help with whatever modest talents he had. Through the long evenings of two winters, Margery confessed her sins and recounted her accomplishments, not in quest of absolution or sympathy, but simply in response to some deep-seated urge to share her experience of life with others who would follow. Finally the task was completed and Margery died quietly in her sleep.

Five hundred years later in the musty gallery, the story came at last to light, the strange tale of a woman who dared to be different.

Lady Pursued Unusual Graduate Study

When men finally accepted the idea that women were intellectually capable of absorbing higher education, near the middle of the last century, the first serious science offered to female students was botany.

The innocent study of plants and flowers, reasoned the men, would keep the girls quietly occupied, while avoiding the danger of hurting themselves or getting into trouble. After all, the pinprick of a thorn or the frightening sight of a wooly worm would seem to be the worst that could happen.

As things turned out, however, a number of women found a way to use the genteel study of botany as a steppingstone to complete, or at least partial, emancipation.

An outstanding example of this urge to escape the prison of womanhood through useful scientific work is found in the story of Mary Kingsley, an English girl, only daughter of a distinguished family.

When Mary's parents died, she set out at age 31 to explore the African Congo alone, planning to study not only flowers and insects but the customs and religion of the people as well.

It was a daring idea in Victorian England, and friends of the family shook their heads in disapproval.

In the year 1893 the lady explorer tramped through the thickest of tropical jungles, living for the most part off the country, but also frequently enjoying the hospitality of native villages.

She spent several weeks as guest of the Great Forest tribes, a people known to be cannibals. On one occasion her hosts provided her with a hut containing some smelly bags, which when emptied turned out to contain a human hand, three big toes, two ears, and a few other items of anatomy.

To win the confidence of the people, Mary posed as a trader, and her stock of beads and hair ribbons helped to insure a warm welcome wherever she went.

But for all her courage, Mary Kingsley was not yet ready to be completely liberated. Even when traveling in the jungle she wore a black dress reaching to her shoetops, a high-necked blouse, and a tight-fitting hat. For protection she carried an umbrella, and of course a hatpin.

One day when approaching a village of thatched huts, Mary stumbled into a tiger trap, a deep pit with bamboo spikes sticking up from the bottom. But because of her long skirt and the voluminous petticoats worn by every respectable Victorian lady, she suffered no injury. Her dignity however was shaken.

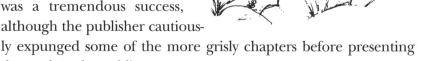

Back in England in 1896, Mary's collection of bugs and plants won the acclaim of the British Museum and the offer of unlimited financing for future work. Her book on life in Africa was a tremendous success, although the publisher cautiously expunged some of the more grisly chapters before presenting the work to the public.

For a couple of years Mary Kingsley basked in the limelight as a celebrity. She lectured on the problems of Africa and its people, warning that European culture should not be imposed by traders and politicians on the Africans. Colonial government, she further urged, should begin with a thorough understanding of African religion, tribal laws and customs.

But sad to say, the story ends in tragedy. When she became disentangled eventually from publishers and speaking engagements, Mary returned to Africa to renew many friendships.

Within a few days she contracted the enteric fever from which so many Africans suffered, and died with the amazing suddenness characteristic of this tropical malady. Mary Kingsley was only 38.

Woman Resurrected as Messiah

In the long history of the Christian faith, the belief arises from time to time that the messiah will return in the form of a woman. This idea is expressed in the strange story of Jemina Wilkinson, a tale which tells how she died as a young girl and arose from her coffin with a new personality.

Jemina Wilkinson was born in 1752 on a farm in Rhode Island. Brought up in a motherless household, the child was wilful, headstrong and romantic. She was singularly beautiful and enjoyed pretty clothes, as well as all the mischief and innocent pleasures of youth.

At age 16, Jemima became deeply interested in religion, and her habits changed overnight. Becoming more moody and temperamental, the young girl spent her days and nights reading religious works and meditating on the nature of salvation. Finally in 1776 her health was impaired. After an illness of several weeks, Jemima went into a coma and was pronounced dead.

Thirty-six hours later, with family and friends assembled for the funeral, the dead girl rose straight up in her coffin and asked for water. From that point she entered into a new life. Completely and suddenly restored to health, Jemima announced that her body had been reanimated by a spirit sent to instruct the world on the proper path to salvation. The name Jemima, she added, was left behind as part of an earlier life, and the title of her new identity was Universal Friend.

While Jemima had been quite small as a child, the world now saw in the Universal Friend a tall graceful figure of radiant beauty. Her manner was warm, endearing, and the magnetism of her personality looked out through piercing, hypnotic eyes.

In this state of restored health and vitality, the Universal Friend began to hold open-air meetings to discuss the salvation of mankind. These gatherings were well attended from the beginning, and many listeners accepted the teachings of the Friend eagerly.

Expanding her mission to wider horizons, the Friend with 20 disciples, traveling on horseback, went on a tour of New England

and Pennsylvania. A few voices of opposition were heard in protest against the doctrine of chastity. Men complained that their wives had grown cold, and that carnal appetites of the flesh could not be suppressed.

Answering a call to go into the wilderness in 1788, the Universal Friend, with several hundred followers, journeyed to the western frontier of New York, to Indian territory where they established the colony of New Jerusalem.

In all, the colony of New Jerusalem consisted of about 300 normal families with their children and about 200 celibate females dedicated to the religious life. For two decades all were contented, peaceful and prosperous, living under the undisputed authority of the Friend.

Then in 1819, to the shock and consternation of her followers, the Universal Friend died — for the second time. For four days a vigil was kept over the body in expectation of a second resurrection. When hope at last died, the body was walled up behind a brick fireplace while plans for a secret burial were completed. This planning was the work of a select few, those who were closest to the Friend in her lifetime.

Only the descendants of those who participated in the burial know to this day where in that lovely valley of New Jerusalem the body of the Universal Friend came at last to its final rest.

For further reading: Dictonary of American Biography, Vol. 10, p. 226 (Scribners, 1936)

Violence Accompanies French Religious Reform

In the history books she is known as Renee of France, and she lived in a time when Europe was torn apart in bitter strife over ideas of religion.

A daughter of the king of France, Renee was born in 1510 and grew up in the royal palace. Her teacher and companion in the early years was an English lady who told the young princess about reforms in the Christian church and new ideas then spreading rapidly. The teacher also shielded the young girl from the immorality prevalent at the time in the French court.

When she reached 18, Renee was married with great ceremony to the Duke of Ferrara, a nobleman from Italy. The couple went to live at a beautiful villa near Rome, and it was here that Renee's five children were born.

As the new ideas about religion spread south from France into Italy, the Ferrara villa became a great center for intellectual discussion. John Calvin, reformist leader who was banished from France, visited there for several weeks and discussed his writings on the changes in religious outlook. But the Duke, Renee's husband, was unsympathetic to the new ideas and had Calvin arrested for heresy, sending him off to prison under armed guard. Renee assembled a stronger group of soldiers to ride in pursuit, and the rescuers escorted Calvin away to a place of safety.

In anger, the Duke took Renee's children from her and humiliated the lady of royal blood by putting her in prison for her offense. When the Duke died in 1559, his will stated that Renee could inherit his fortune only if she abandoned her ideas about religious reform. Renee refused, and her own son, now head of the family, ordered her to leave Italy.

Returning to Paris, Renee found that religious bitterness had reached incredible heights. Bloodshed was now commonplace, while plots and intrigue dominated political life as the great families of France took sides either with the reformists or the traditionalists.

Paris was unsafe, and Renee retired to an old family castle at

Montargis, about 60 miles from the city. Here she established a shelter and a refuge for proponents of the new religious freedom, or Huguenots as these people came to be known in France. When clergymen and families believing in the reformed faith fled from persecution and slaughter in the cities, Renee protected them and fed them in her castle, even providing a chapel where they could worship as they pleased. As many as 300 refugees were sheltered and fed at her table at once.

On St. Bartholomew's Day, August 24, 1572, hundreds of Huguenots were murdered in Paris and elsewhere throughout France by the enemies of religious freedom. Hundreds were saved only because they found refuge behind the walls of Renee's stone castle at Montargis. Repeatedly bands of armed men rode to the gates, but none dared enter.

One of Renee's bitterest enemies was her own son-in-law, the Duke de Guise, a fanatical supporter of the traditionalist cause for political reasons. After St. Bartholomew's Day he ordered that Renee's castle be destroyed stone by stone, until no evidence of its existence remained. On the day that a company of soldiers arrived near the castle to launch their work of destruction, a messenger galloped up to announce that the Duke de Guise had been assassinated in Paris. No one then had the courage to disturb the determined noble lady.

Three years after the infamous slaughter of St. Bartholomew's Day, Renee died quietly in her castle and was buried in the small chapel where she had worshipped for 16 years after her banishment from Italy.

Servant Girl Suffers Persecution

By order of a magistrate she was stripped of her clothing in the public square and whipped until drops of blood stained the cobblestones at her feet. No outcry of pain issues from her lips as she endured her suffering like other Christian visionaries before her.

Youngest daughter of simple peasant parents, Mary Fisher was born in England at a period of great religious unrest, when bigotry and persecution were widespread. When Mary was a small girl growing up, the Puritans were in power, having dislodged the old Established Church in favor of their own rigid, domineering doctrines. Many people of all classes were still in search of an alternative to the old medieval order, a more humane form of Christianity attuned to the realities of life in this world.

As a servant girl in the great house of a noble family, Mary overheard this talk of a new alternative to the cruel, compassionless doctrine of the Puritans, with their unrelenting emphasis on the sinful nature of people and the almost certain fate of an eternity to be spent in the fires of hell. Mary's kindly mistress instructed her in the principles of the new ideas of a Christian life as a means of honoring God in this world by peace and kindness. Soon Mary left her employment to find out more about what she had learned and to spread her little store of knowledge among her own kind of people.

Still in quest of knowledge, Mary arrived at the great city of York where she asked some questions of the Puritan minister in charge.

To her surprise she was promptly thrown in jail, because women were not allowed by Puritans to speak out on any subject of human affairs, religious or otherwise.

During more than a year in prison at York, Mary learned even more from fellow prisoners about the ideas of humane Christianity. When she was at last released in 1653 she set forth with a girl companion to teach what she had learned.

When the two girls attempted to address a group of young Puritan ministerial students, a complaint against them was lodged by the supervisor. It was for this offense of speaking out as women that the two girls were flogged in the market square. As Mary and her companion, blood still dripping from their torn bodies, were led in disgrace to the outskirts of town, people recoiled in horror. News of this barbarous punishment sent a shudder throughout England, the beginning of a national revulsion that would in the end have significant historical consequences.

Mary and her girl companion sailed for Boston in 1656, intent on bringing their news of a Christian belief in harmony with everyday life to the people of the Massachusetts colony. But the Puritan leaders there had been warned of their coming and were determined to reject any preaching of alien doctrines, particularly by women. In Boston harbor, the ship was impounded, then searched from stem to stern. Pamphlets brought with them by the girls were confiscated.

The two women were then imprisoned, in separate cells, deprived of their clothing, with the small single window in each case boarded up to shut out all light. Here the two might have died, but an elderly citizen having heard of their good work, bribed the jailer to let him provide them with food.

Finally Mary's friend was released to make her own way in the Puritan colony. Mary was placed on a ship bound for England. All her belongings, her shoes, her money, her combs and her bonnet, all these were confiscated to pay the jailer's fees, and she sailed for England in a simple one-piece gown.

For 10 more years, Mary Fisher traveled from place to place preaching the text of a simple humane Christianity. Of the hundreds of miles she traveled, most were on foot. Leaving her native England she visited towns and villages in the countries of Europe where Christianity was still in a condition of uncertainty. In time her travels took her to Turkey, a land beyond the bounds of the Christian world. Puzzled peasants in some places regarded her as a kindly mad person. In Constantinople the Sultan of Turkey received her. Politely he listened to her message, but was unimpressed. Instead, noting Mary's fine figure and delicately beautiful features, he invited the visitor to become a member of his harem. Accepting her declination graciously, he assured her of his protection on her journey out of the country.

But life had a reward in store for Mary Fisher after her footsore years of wandering. After a dozen years of pleading against religious persecution, she met a kindred spirit in the person of a ship's captain on the Atlantic route who proposed marriage. She accepted and went on to enjoy nearly 40 years as mother and homemaker, raising two daughters and a son. Until her death as a very old lady in Charleston, S.C., in 1698 she gave all her available time to helping others in community activities.

She Never Knew a Dull Moment

Although the term sex appeal had not yet been invented when she lived her exciting and sinful life, Miriam Follin effectively exploited her natural feminine assets to amass a fortune and a business empire.

Miriam Follin was born at New Orleans in 1836, daughter of a merchant in the import-export business. As a young girl she was sexy and seductive, always craving excitement, and at an early age learned to arouse the attentions of men. In her teen years there was a shot-gun marriage, later annulled, and for a short time she amused herself with a career on the stage.

In 1857 at age 21, Miriam gave up the theater to marry Ephriam Squier, a reporter with the Frank Leslie chain of newspapers and magazines. When Miriam Squier and Frank Leslie met there was an immediate cosmic reaction between the two personalities.

Frank, already separated from his wife, moved in with the newlyweds as a boarder. Ephriam didn't mind since he was frequently absent for days at a time on writing assignments. Sometimes the three traveled together, and once in England Ephriam was arrested for a minor misdemeanor. Frank saw this as a wonderful opportunity to obtain a story on life in British prisons and left Ephriam in jail for two weeks before returning to pay his fine.

This convenient and amicable threesome arrangement continued for more than 10 years as Miriam became Frank's right hand assistant in the publishing buisness.

In due time Frank's absent wife at last died, making him a free man. Miriam immediately demanded a divorce from Ephriam, confronting him with some fabricated evidence of infidelity while absent on assignments. Poor Ephriam literally went out of his mind and soon had to be put away in an institution for the insane.

Now as Mrs. Frank Leslie, Miriam with her furs and jewels became a national sex symbol and an ornament to the great Leslie publishing enterprise. Her face and figure adorned scores of magazine pages and provocative advertising posters. Together the two managed a glittering social life in Europe and America, a glamourous existence which they exploited for business advantage.

Miriam wrote dazzling articles about her travels, about the interesting people they met, knowing that such publicity was good for the circulation of their newspapers and magazines.

When the Leslies appeared at the governor's inaugural ball in 1875 New York was treated to the spectacle of Miriam wearing $70,000 in diamonds. At their palatial country estate they entertained visiting princes and noblemen.

Inevitably the bubble burst. In the business panic of 1877, the great Leslie publishing enterprise collapsed. A day or so later, Frank learned he was in the final stages of a fatal disease. To make matters worse, a rival editor stumbled on the old story of Miriam's brief teenage marriage, along with some titillating details of the threesome household during the years of her marriage to Ephriam.

By the time President Garfield was assassinated in 1898, Frank Leslie publications were back on top scooping the competition under her dynamic female management. Along the way at age 55, Miriam married a smooth and handsome young man of 30 from England, but when she discovered he was no more than a playboy and useless at the office, she promptly divorced him.

Then with things once more going her way Miriam/Frank Leslie sold out the business for $10 million on her 62nd birthday and settled down to enjoy life in retirement.

At 70 she was restless again and contemplated a new marriage, this time with a Spanish nobleman just a year or so older. Unfortunately the groom, perhaps overly excited about his good fortune, passed away on the night before his date at the altar. This was Miriam's last venture into matrimony.

In 1914 when she was 78, the eventful life of this remarkable woman came quietly to an end. She left a substantial share of her fortune to the leadership of the national feminist movement, then at the height of the battle to win the right to vote for women.

Esther Morris Labored for Justice

Because of what she considered a crime against her infant son, Esther Morris became one of the earliest — and one of the most successful — activists in the cause of women's rights. Patient persistence and quiet persuasion were the hallmarks of her long crusade, in contrast with the flamboyant parades and noisy demonstration staged by more aggressive females in later years.

An orphan at age 11, Esther Morris made her own way in the world by sewing hats for the fine ladies of New York. She was married in 1846 at age 28, but two years later found herself a widow with an infant son to support. Hope for the future lay in a modest legacy of property in Illinois left by her deceased husband.

On arriving in Illinois to claim her inheritance, Esther was shocked to discover that women had no legal status in that state. She could not own property, and the legacy left by her husband was worthless to her. A sympathetic lawyer agreed that the law was unjust but the insurmountable barrier of prejudice and tradition made the idea of change unthinkable.

Still a young and attractive woman at age 30, Esther married a storekeeper. The sense of injustice continued to fester in her soul, but years were to pass before the hurt was eased.

When the Civil War came to an end, Esther Morris and her family joined the great population movement to the West, drawn by the multiple magnetism of gold, free land, and a new life. Esther bravely made her home in a shack, one of the community of shacks scattered along the foothills of the Wind River Mountains in Wyoming.

Because of Esther's natural charm and intelligence, the Morris home soon became a community center for women living within a day's ride in the wilderness. Here, over tea and homemade cake, Esther preached her quiet doctrine of equal rights and the necessity for overturning the great barrier of prejudice and tradition. In turn the women carried the message home to their men, softly and subtly, but effectively, as history was to show in the end.

When the first session of the Wyoming Territorial Legislature met in 1869, the young delegate from Sweetwater County introduced a bill granting the right to vote for women in the territory. It was a radical notion for 1869, and the bill was greeted with ridicule, not only in Wyoming but all over the country. Humorists on eastern newspapers had a field day laughing at the ignorant frontiersmen and their childish proposal. But somehow the bill passed, perhaps because tradition and prejudice were as yet without invincible stature in the new country.

In this new climate of freedom and enlightenment, Esther was appointed magistrate to serve the needs of her local community. This event in itself constituted a significant milestone on the path to full equality for women in the life of society — still some years in the future.

Quiet and unassuming as always, the first woman judge in the nation's history held court in her family kitchen, interrupting the household chores when a lawman or posse rode up with a prisoner to be judged.

Esther Morris died in 1902 after winning her long battle against injustice. The community of South Pass in Sweetwater County is now a ghost town crumbling to dust in the shadow of the Wind River Mountains. But the women of America have cause to remember Esther Morris with her determined chin, undaunted persistence, and quiet charm — the lady who drove the entering wedge into the great wall of prejudice and tradition.

Career vs. Motherhood: Is There a Right Answer?

Can a woman be a successful wife and mother while working at a career in the outside world? It is a familiar question, and sometimes the decision can be difficult.

In England about 1800 a wave of social reform was sweeping the country, and it was fashionable for young women to adopt some useful purpose in society. Elizabeth Fry, daughter of a wealthy banker, looked about and decided to work among the poor, teaching their children and visiting their homes in the depressing slums of London.

After two years of this, she married a rich young man when she was 20, and bore him 10 children between 1801 and 1816. (Another came along in 1822.) This feat of motherhood curtailed her good works for a time, although she tried to keep up her visits to the hovels of the poor between pregnancies.

Beginning in 1817, Elizabeth concentrated her energies on Newgate Prison, where she became deeply concerned with conditions and with the treatment of women prisoners, along with the children who, by law and by custom, accompanied their mothers when they were sentenced to spend a tour behind bars. Overcoming the objections of the superintendent, she visited the prisoners daily, hoping to instill a revival of self-respect in the ragged unfortunates milling about within the walls. By her inspirational talks she sought to prepare mothers and children for release into the world that had punished them.

Then disaster struck. As the result of some bad investments, Elizabeth's husband was wiped out financially. The family was destitute, and some means had to be found to provide for the 10 children.

At this point Elizabeth discovered to her dismay that her offspring were utterly undisciplined and unmanageable. In the absence of a mother's guidance and restraint in the home, the children had grown wild, and indeed were virtually as wicked as the slum urchins Elizabeth encountered every day behind prison walls.

A dynamic woman bursting with ideas on betterment of the

world, Elizabeth was now forced to decide what must be done. Should she abandon her career and attempt to repair the wreckage of her family? Or should she continue with her uplifting work which she anticipated, in time, would touch the lives of thousands. Using her gift for tearful persuasion, she then distributed her children to the care of sympathetic if reluctant relatives. By her own account, she experienced a great sense of relief when she had shed the burden of family and returned to her career among the most depraved elements of the city population.

All who knew of her noble work, the hours spent daily in the awesome stench of Newgate, spoke out in admiration. By now the prison superintendent was wholly on her side, since her presence helped suppress violence among his charges.

In the continuing pursuit of her career, Elizabeth visited prisons all over the British Isles and made a report of her findings to a committee of the House of Commons, the first woman to appear before such an august group. Her recommendations contributed materially to efforts then being made to modernize the entire prison system.

As time passed, she extended her work beyond prison walls to visit convict ships in the harbor as they took on their cargoes of abject humanity, male and female, criminals destined for transportation to prison colonies as far away as Australia. In the crowded darkness below decks she spoke to them of hope and the chance of a new life instead of a quick death at the end of a hangman's rope. In due course she became a recognized authority on crime and imprisonment.

As for her own family, its members were never reunited after the initial rupture when the children were small. Elizabeth by her decision gave up the warmth of the family circle and the satisfaction of seeing her children develop and grow under her eyes. Instead she gave all her strength, her time, and her eloquence to strangers.

Did she ever regret the decision? Did she ever wonder if her career was worth what she had sacrificed? Nobody knows. When she died at age 65, there was no one at her bedside to hold her hand or ask her the question.

White House Visit Inspires Lofty Dream

When Nellie Herron was seventeen, she and her sister were overnight guests of First Lady Lucy Hayes at the White House. The reason for the presence of the two girls from Ohio in Washington is long since forgotten, but Nellie was so impressed by the experience that she made up her mind about her own future.

Some day, she vowed to herself, she would live in the White House as First Lady in her own right.

With this lofty objective in mind, Nellie took her time about shopping for a husband. It was not until 1886, when she was 25, that she married William Howard Taft, a young judge and a member of an old Cincinnati family.

But William had no particular desire to be President. Easygoing, chubby, and inclined to be lazy, he liked being a judge and did not want to be anything else.

However, with wifely persistence, Nellie nudged him along over the years until his name was well-known in Ohio politics and he became one of the most prominent judges in the country.

After the Spanish-American War, President Roosevelt appointed Taft governor of the Philippines, a job which pleased William since the position was really a high-level judicial assignment. Nellie glowed as First Lady of the islands, but never forgot her initial target.

Then with the Philippine assignment completed, there followed in 1906 a momentous interview with President Roosevelt in the White House. When dinner had been cleared away and everyone was comfortably relaxed, the President offered Taft his choice of two possible appointments: Republican candidate for President in 1906 or a lifetime seat as a justice of the U. S. Supreme Court.

"The Supreme Court," answered William promptly.

"The Presidency," countered Nellie firmly.

In the push and pull of several months following, Nellie's iron will, backed by years of determination, prevailed over the resistance of her 350-pound husband. Taft won the Presidency in 1908, thus fulfilling Nellie's lifetime ambition.

Nellie was the first woman to ride in the open carriage beside her husband in the inaugural parade from the Capitol to the White

House. In addition, the Tafts were the first Presidential couple to use an automobile, which was parked in the White House stable with the horses.

A permanent reminder of Nellie and her delight in being First Lady can still be seen in the nation's capital. It was she who arranged for planting the hundreds of cherry trees which continue to beautify the avenues of the city every spring.

Eight years after the Tafts left the White House, President Harding offered William a seat on the Supreme Court. When he accepted promptly and gladly, there was no word of objection this time from Nellie.

She Chose the Life of a Wild West Outlaw

The girl who became known as the last of the big-time female outlaws in the Old West was not born for a life of crime and violence. Her story shows how evil men, intent only on their own pleasure, can lead a respectable girl into the paths of sin.

Myra Belle Shirley was born at Carthage, Mo., where her family owned a prosperous hotel. At age eight, Myra Belle enrolled in the Carthage Academy for Young Ladies, where she studied Latin, Greek, mathematics and music. After the Civil War erupted, Union troops burned down the Shirley Hotel, and the family moved to Texas, to a small community near Dallas. It was here that Myra Belle grew up to be a succulent flower of young womanhood.

When a childhood sweetheart from Missouri came all the way to Texas to plead for Myra's hand, the family rejoiced. Already the fires of desire were alight in the breast of the beautiful maiden, and there were but few desirable suitors among the rough Texas frontiersmen. So with full family blessing, James Reed claimed his bride and carried her proudly back to Missouri.

But unknown to Myra Belle at first, James Reed was a lawless man in a lawless country. Once back in his native Missouri he joined up with a band of outlaws known as the Starr gang. Myra soon learned that she was expected to tie up gunshot wounds for her husband's criminal friends. Watering and grooming of sweaty horses became routine chores for her delicate hands, while occasionally exhausted unwashed bandits slept in her bed.

After six years of this nightmare existence, and the birth of two children, Myra was no longer the cultured young ornamental lady she had been on her wedding day. Then on a day when her fleeing husband was shot to death by a deputy sheriff, her cup of bitterness was filled to overflowing.

Desolate in her grief and ashamed to return to her parents, Myra gave her children away and wandered for a time through the glittering saloons and gambling halls of the frontier West. Because of her intelligence and education, she found ready employment as a card dealer, and because of her beauty and charm, men fought for the privilege of her company.

Lonely and discouraged, she accepted the attentions of one suitor after another, and very quickly her personality became calloused. By age 30, Myra Belle was a woman without love, without conscience and without honor.

In 1880 she married 22-year-old Sam Starr, son of the leader of the notorious Starr gang. Thus the girl who was born Myra Belle Shirley was now on the way to becoming the infamous Belle Starr, a heartless criminal who attained new heights of notoriety as "The Lady Desperado," "The Bandit Queen" and "The Petticoat Terror of the Plains."

Destined to follow in her new husband's footsteps, the young woman began her career of evil with a flair. Not only did she participate in some of the most daring crimes of her day, but she did so bedecked in the finery of a true lady.

On forays of robbery at the head of the gang, she rode sidesaddle on a fine black mare, wearing a velvet gown and with a long plume flowing from her hat. A reward of $10,000 in gold was offered for her capture, dead or alive.

When her husband Sam went to prison to serve a short sentence, Myra simply transferred her attentions to other men, and here was her undoing. Several gun duels were fought over her favors, but Myra felt no sorrow, no compassion and refused to commit herself to any exclusive alliance. Anger and suspicion spread among members of the gang, so that any semblance of brotherhood or loyalty was soon shattered.

As tension mounted jealousy was the dominant emotion among men, but Belle laughed in scorn. Little did she realize that jealously is only a whisper removed from hate. On a spring morning in 1889 when riding her black mare, Myra was gunned down by a shotgun blast fired by a jealous lover. Heartlessly he left her to die in the dust at the edge of the trail.

Of a dozen suspects questioned by the sheriff, none could definitely be accused of the crime. So ended the troubled life of Belle Starr, a victim of lustful men. She was just a little more than 40 when she breathed her last.

Her Message Carried the Promise of a Better Life

With all the emphasis these days on family planning and freedom of choice for women, it seems a shame that the name of Margaret Sanger is no longer mentioned. Millions of young women today have never heard of her. But without the pioneering efforts of the determined lady, her submission to insult and indignity along with her willingness to go to jail, the whole area of family planning would still be stuck in the Dark Ages. As a matter of fact it was Margaret Sanger who invented the term "birth control" to begin with.

Margaret Sanger was born in 1883, the sixth in a family of 11 children. She studied nursing in New York and became an obstetrical nurse in the dismal lower East Side of Manhattan. Here she was shocked by the mortality rates of young wives who gave birth to six, eight, or a dozen children as quickly as nature would permit. The turning point came in her life when a young girl died in her arms from a self-induced abortion. From this experience Margaret Sanger set out to emancipate women from what she called the Curse of Eve, the servitude of unwanted pregnancy.

Historical records dating back to ancient Egypt and Greece contain references to contraceptive practices employed for a variety of reasons — economic considerations, for example, or improvement in the fighting qualities of soldiers by refinement of the genetic makeup. Margaret Sanger ignored all motives but one as she dedicated her life to promoting the idea of freedom of choice as a basic human right that should be available to all women.

In defiance of a New York law prohibiting the dissemination of information on contraception, she opened the first birth control clinic in the United States at a vacant store in the poorest section of Brooklyn. Police promptly raided the clinic and arrested its founder. Released on bail, Margaret Sanger promptly reopened, and the arrest performance was repeated half a dozen times. At last the police desisted, awaiting a verdict from the courts, but continuing surveillance by patrols frightened many clients away.

Simple pamphlets on family planning distributed to the poor were declared pornographic and banned for a time from the mails.

Neighborhood toughs, sensing a threat to their masculine domination over women, lounged on the corner near the clinic making lewd remarks to those entering or leaving the premises. Obscene insults were chalked on the windows and doors.

Even some of the women themselves were suspicious of the clinic, wondering why anyone should be concerned enough to help them. Many residents of the bedraggled streets were immigrant Jews from Europe, and a rumor was circulated that the whole thing was a dastardly plot to wipe out the Jewish race by restricting births.

But perseverance prevailed. A few wealthy persons supported the Sanger crusade with money but discreetly declined to give the public endorsement of their names. In 1917, with the help of some elements of the women's liberation movement, Margaret Sanger founded the National Birth Control League, which later became the Planned Parenthood Federation of America. A decade later came the first International Birth Control Congress at Geneva in 1927.

Culmination of a rewarding career came in 1952 when the International Planned Parenthood Federation was established under auspices of the U.N. with Margaret Sanger as its first president.

Few women have done as much to advance the cause of women's liberation, and there is no way of knowing how many lives have been saved as a result of her work. But the world, alas, is quick to forget. Only a dozen years have passed since her death*, and already it seems that she is forgotten. Maybe somebody some day will remember and build a monument.

*written 1978

She Found that the World Can Indeed Be Cruel

Marie Bouvier was born in 1648 just outside Paris. As a teenager she was very beautiful, but inclined to be vain and frequently wore daring and provocative gowns at social affairs. On her 16th birthday, she married a man of wealth and social position, but 22 years older.

Not until after the wedding did Marie discover that her husband was a semi-invalid, subject to terrifying seizures and periodic loss of his faculties.

A nurse was maintained on the household staff to care for the sick man, and this nurse despised the new bride. In addition, Marie soon learned that her mother-in-law did not approve of the marriage. Thus the two older women conspired together to make life miserable for the interloper.

They permitted her no authority over household affairs. They humiliated her before the servants and their sharp tongues never ceased to stab and slash at their young victim.

But Marie was a faithful wife and dutifully presented her husband with four children as the cycles of nature would permit. Then in a year when smallpox was widespread in France, the oldest boy caught the dread disease. Marie herself nursed him, holding the small body in her arms through sleepless nights and feverish days.

The child died, and even as he breathed his last in her embrace, Marie realized that she too had become infected with the hated pox.

In due course Marie recovered, but her face and body were left horribly scarred by the characteristic marks of the disease. Her beauty was ruined.

The face that had once turned the heads of men in Paris was now the visage of a monster. Neither her mother-in-law nor her husband's nurse offered any word of comfort or consolation.

Alas, the cup of her bitterness was not yet filled. When Marie was 28, her sick husband sank into a coma during one of his seizures. Faithful to the end, the young wife knelt at his bedside as life ebbed away and then disappeared. On the day of the funeral Marie's mother-in-law announced that the young widow and her children were no longer welcome in the family home.

In attempting to build a new life with her surviving children, Marie learned more about human cruelty. Merchants were repelled by her ugliness, and some shops refused to serve her. In school her children were taunted as the offspring of a witch.

Finally after five years of this intolerable existence, Marie sorrowfully placed her children in a convent and set out to find peace alone.

In this new crisis she turned to religion, not the simple conventional Christianity of her childhood, but a strange mystical belief that salvation could be found only in direct, personal communication with God.

Obsessed by this belief, Marie set forth to preach the doctrine of mystical personal unity to audiences all over Europe. She wore a hood to conceal her ugliness and a single full length smock of coarse cloth. Perhaps because of her strange, almost supernatural appearance, she attracted large crowds on city streets and in rural village squares.

Presently, church leaders became jealous of her ability to draw so many listeners to her unconventional ideas. She was accused of being a heretic, a mad person and a woman of low moral character. Time after time, she was imprisoned for persisting in her mission, and in 1698 was committed to four years solitary confinement at the Bastile, the notorious prison in Paris.

During this time she wrote down the story of her life, as well as the details of the strange relationship she claimed to have with the Supreme Being.

Finally in 1702, the King of France paroled her, but banished her to a small village and barred her from entering the city again.

In this rustic retreat, isolated from the world, Marie continued to put her thoughts on paper as she approached the end of her 69 years. Repeatedly she emphasized she had no wish to be remembered by the world after her death. Scholars still read the manuscripts she left, the story of one woman's sorrowful existence in a cruel and heartless world.

The Bread Lady of New Orleans

A simple person with no education whatever, Margaret Haughery proved that a lone woman can attain success in a cruel world — without any help from the opposite sex.

Her early life was a succession of one tragedy after another. Margaret came to America from Ireland as a small girl with her impoverished immigrant parents. In 1822, when Margaret was nine, both parents caught yellow fever and died quickly. A priest arranged for the child to be adopted by foster parents in New Orleans, but because Margaret was too frail for heavy domestic work they soon turned her out on the streets to make her own way.

For a time the skinny girl washed clothes, or peeled potatoes and cleaned fish in a hotel kitchen. At age 15 she tried marriage, but the sickly man of her choice passed away within weeks. Margaret's only source of hope in those years was in the work of the nuns of New Orleans who struggled to feed the poor. Grateful for their help in her extremity, Margaret determined that one day she would share in this noble task.

Saving every penny she possibly could from her paltry earnings, Margaret eventually bought two small cows, and in a handcart borrowed from the convent, began peddling milk in the city streets. She kept the animals in an old abandoned shed that was supposed to be haunted. People passing on the nearby road were sometimes frightened by the shadows of Margaret and her lantern tending to her cows in the dead of the night. By day the animals grazed along ditch banks, subsisting on the green fodder provided by nature.

Because of her reliability and her attention to cleanliness, Margaret's milk business prospered tremendously. By 1840, when she was 27, the enterprising young woman owned 40 cows and was delivering milk in the fashionable new uptown neighborhood of New Orleans. As new employees were needed to keep up with the growing business, Margaret gave preference as much as possible to orphan children who were so numerous on the city streets. When money gradually became more plentiful, Margaret poured more help into the orphanages operated by the nuns and other charitable groups.

In 1842, Margaret took over a bankrupt bakery that could not pay its milk bills, and soon turned it once more into a profitable undertaking. Steam power was new at the time, but Margaret had the vision to see how new equipment could be put to use. Then she combined the milk and bread services so that fresh milk and bread were delivered daily to all the best homes in New Orleans. Orphanages received bread and milk free.

Margaret became an important person in the city, not only because she now had money but because she had a natural talent for management, a quality rare among men and even rarer among women. Scores of people came to her for advice and assistance, including prominent businessmen who respected her for her success in making money. When the War Between the States came along, it was Margaret who organized extensive nursing services to care for wounded soldiers.

With the passage of years Margaret continued to expand her business. Cookies packed for export became a major cargo for the port of New Orleans. Nobody ever knew how much money she made. She kept that information to herself, and lived quietly with no outward display of wealth. Like other widows of the time, she always dressed in black, and owned only two dresses, one for weekdays and one for Sundays.

When she died at age 70 Margaret left all her considerable estate to the 11 orphanages and homes for the aged she had founded. Because in all her busy life of hard work and consideration for others she had never learned to read or write she signed her will with a large X which the court accepted as legal and binding. Her response to her own early poverty and loneliness was to make the poor and unfortunate her own special family. Thus ends the simple story of the kindly person known to hundreds of children as the Bread Lady of New Orleans.

Imagination Built A Fortune

Nell Curtis Demorest was never a ravishing beauty, but she had a vivid imagination. Nell was born in 1824, only child of an upstate New York factory owner. When the young girl reached marriagable age, with no prospective suitors in sight, her father set her up in business with a small hat shoppe, an appropriate occupation for an old maid.

Then when Nell was 33, a fast-talking young fellow from New York City breezed into town and swept her off her feet. A resourceful fellow with irons in the fire and things to do, Will Demorest married the girl, closed up the shoppe and whisked her off to a new life in the big city.

Husband Will was an inventor and a promoter, always in search of new ideas. Nell soon caught inventive fever. One day while watching her maid cut up some wrapping paper for a dress pattern, inspiration struck. Of course housewives had been cutting out paper patterns for years, but now for the first time Nell thought of the idea of precut patterns, to be cut by experts and sold. Isaac Singer's new sewing machine was becoming popular with American women, and the precut paper pattern would make dressmaking quicker and easier. Clothes would fit better, with more accurate sizes, but even more important, the precut pattern would make top-quality design available to every amateur dressmaker.

Husband Will was enthusiastic. The aristocratic styles of rich women and French couturiers could be brought into every home by means of a few scraps of tissue paper. Thus a new industry, fashion as distinct from clothes, came into being. Because so many of the new fashions came from France, Nell changed her name from Mrs. William Demorest to Madame Demorest.

Before long Nell had a score of women cutting patterns and packing them in envelopes. More than 200 local agents — widows and spinsters — sold the patterns through 300 distribution agencies throughout the country. By 1873 sales were more than two million patterns a year.

At the height of her enthusiasm, Nell started a magazine to

promote her business. It was called, "Madame Demorest's Mirror of Fashion," and was mainly a picture book of dresses a woman could make at home with Nell's patterns. In her magazine, Nell also started the very first column of advice to women, writing under the name of Jeannie June. As the forerunner of Ann Landers and Dear Abby, Jeannie June was an outspoken feminist, advocating equality of the sexes in marriage, education, employment and the professions. When other feminists were agitating for the right to vote, Jeannie June urged women to go into business, to make money, and offered practical advice on how to do it. The first real women's club in America, the Sorosis, was founded by Jeannie June and her readers.

Meanwhile, husband Will, happily watching the money pour in, offered some of his inventions for sale in the magazine. One was the "Imperial Dress Elevator," a device with weighted strings which enabled a lady to raise or lower the hem of her skirt as she mounted a sidewalk or negotiated a puddle. Another was an aid to glamour called the "Spiral Spring Bosom Pad."

So the lady who was once an old maid running a small-town hat shoppe was now a national and international figure in the world of fashion. She had an exclusive New York emporium for the social upper crust and a mail order shopping service for women, offering hats, hairpieces, shoes, jewelry, parasols and all the other hallmarks of civilization. She visited Paris once a year, and in New York presided over her own fashion shows.

For all their success, Nell and husband Will made one fatal mistake. In the exciting years when so much was happening they neglected to patent the magic fundamental idea of precut dress patterns. Somewhere along the line, a small dry-goods merchant in Massachusetts began peddling his own precut patterns by mail and had the foresight to secure a patent on the process. Of course a great court battle with the Demorest empire eventually ensued, but Nell, with no patent and no proof that she thought of the idea first, lost the case.

The little man from Massachusetts was named Ebenezer Butterick, and the company bearing his name still dominates the pattern market up to the present day. But dear Nell should not be forgotten. Some say she built her fortune on the vanity of the female sex, and be that as it may, she demonstrated that Judy O'Grady and the colonel's lady are sisters under the skin.

This French Heroine Saved Many from Massacre

In the French province of Normandy, Charlotte Corday was born in 1763, daughter of a noble family reduced to poverty by heavy taxation. Since her father could not afford to maintain three daughters, he gave Charlotte in adoption at age 13 to an elderly aunt. The aunt hoped that, in exchange for a home and education, the girl would be a comfort to her in old age.

They lived quietly together, these two women separated in age by so many years. Charlotte accompanied her aunt to church and on errands about the village. Otherwise she spent most of her days reading for hours in the courtyard near the fountain.

France as a nation at that time was drifting rapidly toward revolution. People were tired of a king who ruled as he pleased and imposed heavy taxes for his luxurious living. At first the revolution began in 1789 as orderly reform, but the movement soon degenerated into violence in all the cities of France.

When a political party called the Girondists took power in 1791, the wave of terror became worse as hundreds of people from the best families in France were executed every day. Hired gangs, inflamed by free wine, roamed the streets in an orgy of bloodshed, plunder and rape. It was said that France as a nation had lost her self-respect.

In her Normandy garden, Charlotte read of all these things and was deeply distressed.

Finally in January 1793, Marat's revolutionaries executed the king and queen of France in a drunken public spectacle. Charlotte decided then what she had to do. She was 24 years old.

Her plan was simple. In Paris Charlotte called on a number of minor Girondist officials offering information on people in Normandy who were disloyal to the new regime. But these names were so important, she insisted, that they should be given only to someone of higher rank. In this way she obtained letters of introduction to officials at successively higher levels, until at last she had an introduction to the great Jean Paul Marat himself.

It was dusk when Charlotte came to the apartment where Marat lived. At the door Marat's wife said the great man was busy and could see no one. But Marat, overhearing the voices — and having already heard of the beautiful girl from Normandy with important information — shouted to let her come in.

Marat was in his bath, a long iron tub placed in the center of the room. A board across the sides of the tub served as a desk where the doctor worked on his papers while he soaked. Standing over him, Charlotte acknowledged his greeting. Then, choosing her moment, she pulled a long knife from her cloak and plunged it deep into his heart. Blood gushed forth to mingle with the bath water, and in seconds the tyrant was dead.

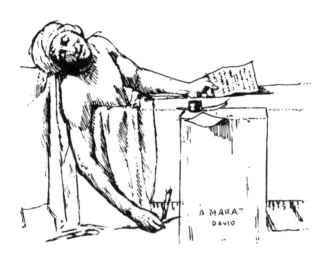

She Climbed a Long, Steep Ladder to Professional Distinction

No doubt the name of Florence Ellinwood Allen means little or nothing to the generation of young women growing up in America today. But the story of her rise to eminence in a profession dominated from time immemorial by men provides an inspiring example of the value of female determination and a firm faith in one's principles.

For the first 25 years of her life Florence Allen fluttered about from one activity to another in an attempt to find a sense of direction for the future. She was born in Salt Lake City in 1884, a primitive frontier community at the time with no formal school system and very little in the way of material comforts. As a result of intensive tutoring by her scholarly father, Florence was ready to leave home for college at age 16, and bravely took a train for the East in pursuit of higher education.

Although women in college were still widely regarded as oddities of the feminine sex, Florence proved to be an outstanding student and earned warm respect from faculty and her associates. Following graduation she supported herself by teaching music for a while. Then she drifted through a brief career in journalism, while writing some poetry and toying with the idea of becoming an architect. Living in the congestion of the city, Florence soon became aware of social injustice, of discrimination against the poor and oppressed. Out of her concern she conceived the idea of working for the improvement of life through law, and making up her mind to become a lawyer, Florence at last found her sense of direction in life.

Unfortunately the thought proved easier than the deed. No law school in the country would admit a woman at the time. Finally her perseverance and patience won out. Florence Allen in 1912 became the first woman to graduate from the law school at New York University.

For the next few years, since no clients came to her office, the young lawyer devoted her talents to defending the poor and to providing legal services to the women's suffrage movement. She defended demonstrators arrested for disturbing the peace, wrote briefs for actions against election commissions. In support for an unpopular cause she became the first woman to address the state supreme court of Ohio, and her sincere dedication won the respect of the legal-judicial establishment.

Then in 1920 American women at last won the right to vote, and Florence Allen became a sort of symbol of emancipation for the women of Ohio. In that first year when the female crusaders were entitled to a voice at the polls, Florence Allen was elected Judge of the Court of Common Pleas by the largest majority ever given a candidate for that office. As a judge she proved to be just, imaginative and compassionate. Speaking now with a voice of authority she initiated a wave of reforms which removed many of the archaic impediments to justice in the state court system.

As testimony to public approval for her methods and goals, Florence was elected to the State Supreme Court in 1922, first woman in the world ever to sit on a court of last resort. Her career reached a distinguished climax in 1934 when President Franklin D. Roosevelt appointed her a judge on the U.S. Court of Appeals, the first and only woman in the world to serve in that capacity.

In a busy life devoted to the welfare of others, Florence Allen found no time for marriage and a family. As she approached the twilight of her years, she enjoyed a graceful old age with her books, her flowers, and her lifelong love for music. A fearless fighter for social justice, Florence Allen opened doors previously closed to women and provided a beacon of inspiration for those who would follow in her footsteps.

She Explored the Horror of Hell on Earth

A pioneer in the great wave of social reform that swept America in the 19th century, this lady became a tireless crusader for humane treatment of those stricken by mental or emotional disturbances.

Dorothea Dix was born in 1802 at a one-room cabin in the Maine wilderness, daughter of parents who were both considered unstable. Her father, earlier expelled from Harvard, was a fanatical traveling preacher, addicted to drink. Her mother spent most of her time in bed suffering from imaginary illnesses.

When Dorothea was 14, her grandmother brought her into her home at Boston and found work for her at a nearby school. In the teaching career which followed, Dorothea formed many friendships among prominent Bostonians who would be helpful in later years.

In 1836, at age 34, Dorothea suffered a physical and emotional breakdown from overwork. Recovery was slow, but life was eased by a small inheritance left by her deceased grandmother. During the long months of convalescence, she wondered about the treatment of disturbed persons who had neither friends nor money.

Upon investigation Dorothea was horrified to discover that in Massachusetts at that time, paupers, criminals and the insane were all confined together, as if all were equally guilty. Since the insane were believed to be possessed by the devil, their treatment was particularly harsh, and some jailers believed it was their Christian duty to punish these deranged creatures who were no longer regarded as human beings.

In the Cambridge jail where Dorothea read the Bible regularly to inmates, she found men and women, naked and thin as shadows, confined in underground dungeons without light or ventilation. Some were chained in medieval fashion to iron rings in the wall, and their only bed was the damp stone floor.

Deeply distressed by what she had found, Dorothea pleaded with three prominent Boston gentlemen to do something. They listened sympathetically, promising that if she could produce evidence showing this to be a general condition, they would bring the matter up in the state legislature.

For the next 18 months, Dorothea, notebook in hand, spent her waking hours visiting scores of jails and other public institutions, and finding unspeakable horror at every turn. At one place she found a woman, who seemed to be perfectly sane, tied up in a dark stall like a farm animal. No one could remember why she had been put there or why her clothing had been taken from her. Her bed was a sprinkling of straw spread on the dirt.

In other places Dorothea saw arms and legs pinioned, necks bowed beneath iron fetters. She saw men and women in cages and listened to screams emanating from behind locked doors while jailers shrugged in indifference.

True to their word, Dorothea's influential friends presented her report to the state legislature with the demand that changes be made. Opposition was substantial. Jailers denied the charges, and many citizens could not believe the horrors described in Dorothea's report. But the nobler instincts of humanity prevailed, and the state of Massachusetts appropriated $200,000 in 1843 for a central mental hospital.

For Dorothea this triumph was but a beginning. Now a thin middle-aged lady wearing a bonnet and a shawl, she set out on a crusade that would cover 30,000 miles from Canada to the Gulf of Mexico and west to the Mississippi. She spoke to everyone who would listen, pleading in her gentle voice for more humane treatment of the unfortunate. Opposition gradually gave way to growing support.

In New Jersey in 1845 a state senator asked the legislature for an appropriation of $1,000 to "transport this meddlesome female across the Delaware River and out of the state." Instead New Jersey built a great mental hospital at Trenton which was to become a model for the rest of the nation.

One after another of state legislatures responded to her appeal, enacting laws to build adequate mental hospitals and improving those already in existence. Following Massachusetts and New Jersey, Illinois and Pennsylvania were next to follow her recommendations, and the winds of change began to sweep through the South.

Through the years she carried her message of compassion from place to place, interrupting her travels only long enough to serve as a nurse in the Civil War. By 1881, now 79 years old, she was tired and went for a rest to the model hospital at Trenton. Here the board of governors set aside a roomy and comfortable apartment for her use. Here she ended her days in peace.

Lady Pirate Dares To Be Different

This red-headed lady buccaneer was more ferocious than any masculine pirate who ever sailed the seven seas. Her exploits struck terror in the hearts of honest seamen from the West Indies and the American coast to the shores of France and Spain.

Anne Bonny was born about 1695 at a small seaport town in Ireland. In a community where most young men went off to sea at an early age, Anne and her playmates growing up found that suitors were scarce.

When she was 19, Anne married an old man, captain of a coastal trading vessel, and joined him to share his life in the cramped quarters of the ship's cabin. The vivacious red-headed girl soon found existence unbearably dull on board ship. There was no dancing or recreation of any kind, and her husband, although kindly, was undeniably old.

Then handsome young Danny Rackman joined the ship as first mate, and Anne took notice at once. Even in the first few days their eyes seemed to meet at every turn. Presently one night in the shadow of the wheelhouse, the two plotted to steal the ship and set out to make a new life of their own. Next day when the captain was ashore on business, Danny hoisted a sail, and the ship slipped quietly out of the harbor.

For the next five years Danny and Anne roamed the seas as operators of a pirate ship, attacking merchant vessels wherever they found them. Their crew was composed of jailbirds and murderers recruited from the drinking dens of a dozen seaports.

In the many battles they fought, Anne was always in front of the action, with a pistol in one hand and a long knife in the other. When prisoners were captured, it was she who decided their fate, either a quick walk on the plank to a watery grave or consignment to float on the ocean in an open boat. The fortunate few of these who were rescued by passing ships spread lurid tales of Anne Bonny, the red-haired lady buccaneer.

But Anne's bold aggressiveness in a world of men proved to be her undoing. Danny, as captain, issued all instructions to the crew on routine operations of the ship, but all knew well that the lady was really in charge. Behind his back, the pirates sneered at Danny for being dominated by a woman. Once as a sign of derision, the men hoisted a woman's petticoat to the top of the mast instead of a flag.

As a result of all this, discipline became lax. Men became careless about their duties. Guards sometimes drank rum or slept on duty. Disaster was inevitable. When the pirate ship dropped anchor to rest in the quiet seclusion of a tropical cove, Danny and Anne woke next morning to see a British war frigate lying in wait for them at the entrance to the harbor. They were trapped.

When British marines swarmed aboard the pirate ship, a hand-to-hand battle ensued. Anne as usual was the most daring fighter of all, with pistol in one hand and knife in the other. However, within minutes, she looked about the deck to find that she was alone. Danny and the pirate crew had fled below decks to escape the swinging blades of British swords. The battle was over. When Danny presently emerged on deck, under guard and with his arms tied, Anne flung the empty pistol at his head. "Coward!" she shrieked. "If you had fought like a man, you would not now have to hang like a dog." And Danny indeed was hanged immediately by order of the British captain.

Anne pleaded that she was pregnant and asked that the life of her unborn child be spared. Accordingly, the British captain transported her all the way across the ocean to be lodged in an English jail. There after sufficient time had passed to prove her claim of pregnancy false, a stern judge told her: "You cannot commit the crimes of a man and expect to escape punishment to be hanged by the neck,"

So Anne too was hanged on Gallows Hill as a common pirate and an enemy of the King. Thus ended the short and tragic life of a woman who — cheated of romance as a girl — tried to find freedom and self-fulfillment in a world created by men.

Mountains Will Move

With all the excitement over a female running for vice president, everyone seems to have forgotten that exactly a hundred years ago in 1884 the nation had a woman candidate for President of the United States. This lady was no crackpot or feminist freak, but a legitimate, respectable contender with better qualifications than any of the men in the race.

Belva Ann Lockwood was born in the 1830s at a small rural community in upstate New York. She grew up with a profound belief in the teachings of the Bible and the unlimited power of personal faith. At about age ten, she attempted to walk on water but received a spanking when she got home with skirts and pantalets soaked with the ooze of a muddy pond. In later life she observed that with time she had indeed learned to move mountains through the power of faith and determination.

When she was 14, Belva received her first introduction to the realities and injustices of life. A bright and obedient child, she was selected to teach in the local schoolroom at a salary of $5 per month plus board at the preacher's home. Soon she discovered that the other teacher, a young boy about her own age, was paid $10 for the same work. Belva complained to the wife of the Methodist minister and was told simply, "Be quiet, child; that is the way of the world." This shock was the genesis and the source of energy for a long and remarkable career that would lead to affluence and distinction in the world of law and politics.

Through the years of her youth Belva devoted herself to education as the only gateway of release from the prison of being born a woman. After obtaining a degree from Genesee College in three years, she was appointed principal of Lockport Union School, a choice assignment at $400 per year. Here again frustration awaited when she learned that her male assistant earned $600. But Belva saved her pennies and in due course opened her own seminary for girls where she taught such unladylike subjects as gymnastics and public speaking. By 1866 she had enough money to move to Washington where she opened the first coeducational private school. Ten years later, Belva Ann was a successful lawyer and somewhat of a thorn in the side of the legal profession.

As a practicing lawyer, Belva Lockwood was champion of the poor and oppressed, leaving more lucrative cases to money-hungry male colleagues. But money and honors nevertheless came her way, in spite of the mountains that had to be moved along the way. When she was nominated as candidate for President by the National Equal Rights Party in 1884, she was much too sensible to think she could win. But she accepted in the belief that even one electoral vote for a woman would be a major milestone for equal rights. (Susan B. Anthony and her flock, incidentally, were shamefully silent.)

Historians have described the presidential campaign of 1884 as the dirtiest on record. Democrat Grover Cleveland, eventual winner, was reputed to have a secret illegitimate child hidden in his background. The Republican was widely denounced in rhyme as, "James G. Blaine, continental liar from the state of Maine." Benjamin Butler of the Greenback party was also known as "Spoons" Butler for his role in stealing the family silver from citizens of New Orleans when assigned as military governor there. The mud slingers could find no exploitable scandal in Belva's past, but the campaign produced many friends who could have been mistaken for enemies.

The lady personally drew up the party platform and conducted an extensive tour of speaking engagements. Her meetings were well attended, and multitudes of voters were sincerely impressed by her innovative proposals and her command of national issues. So impressed were some communities that men wearing Mother Hubbards (women's housecoats) and sunbonnets paraded through the streets bearing brooms, dustpans, and other items of everyday household utility.

Some groups went so far as to wear the high-button shoes then fashionable for ladies. The idea they hoped to convey was that Belva as President would clean house of all the corruption that had characterized national government since the close of the Civil War. The newspapers naturally gave ample display space to these colorful parades.

On election day 1884, Belva and the Equal Rights Party garnered 4,149 votes in six states; all, of course, cast by men. At some precincts in Pennsylvania, hoodlums dumped her votes in waste baskets, and Indiana wanted to change its mind in her favor after voting first for Cleveland. This was not to be.

In the years to follow, honors were heaped on her aging head. The State Department assigned her to all sorts of international meetings. Colleges jostled each other in competition to award her honorary degrees, and her lecture engagements provided comfortably for financial needs.

Commenting in old age on her eventful career, Belva remembered herself in upstate New York as "a little dirty-faced girl...not afraid of snakes or rats or nothing, could walk a rail fence for a mile without falling off, and loved to ride the horses after the cows."

As for her political career and the prospect of a woman someday becoming President of the United States—well, walking on water might be easier.

For further reading: Who's Who in America, 1916-17, New York Times, May 20, 1917

She Made Lots of Money with Her Magical Medicine

When Lydia Estes was married in 1843 she soon discovered that her husband was not a good provider. Poor Isaac tried hard enough, but everything he touched seemed to turn to mud.

First, he was in the shoe business, operating a small factory which failed. Using what money he could salvage from that, he then went into the real estate business with disastrous results. For a while after that he sold plows, harness and buggies.

Over the years as their five children came along, the family moved from one place to the next, each habitation a little shabbier than the last. Finally after 30 years of marriage, during another family crisis, Lydia decided they had reached a dead end. Isaac was broke again, but this time he owed so much money he had to keep out of sight.

In seeking a solution to the problem, Lydia looked within herself. For years as wife and mother, she had cured all her family's ailments, and those of the neighbors, with her own homemade medicines. Lydia knew too that most of the women in the community disliked and distrusted doctors with their irreverent probing fingers and nosy personal questions. Since most doctors of the day knew little of the mysteries of the female anatomy, they often did more harm than good anyway.

Now with the help of her two oldest boys and a copper kettle, Lydia decided to go into the medicine business, catering particularly to the multitudinous disorders of the female sex. Isaac could not help since he spent most of his time in the woods in those days, hiding from his creditors.

Next, Lydia reduced all her medical knowledge and experience down to a single formula that would serve all purposes. There was nothing secret about it. The ingredients were scattered about the kitchen table for anyone to see — unicorn root, fenugreek seed, black cohosh and a few other things. These ingredients were cooked and blended in the kettle, then bottled in a 20 percent solution of alcohol which served as a preservative.

Success was immediate, beyond anything Lydia had hoped or anticipated. Women flocked from far and wide to buy supplies of the magic medicine. Lydia ordered printed labels modestly reading. "The Greatest Medical Discovery Since the Dawn of History."

As sales continued to soar, Lydia became convinced that her medicine was the salvation of the world, and she was the savior. She wrote most of the advertising, saying, "only a woman can understand a woman's ills." When a few ladies testified that the medicine had brought an end to years of sterility, Lydia produced a new label, "A Baby in Every Bottle."

Someone then suggested that Lydia put her picture on the bottle, and she had a special photograph made for the purpose. This somehow added a personal touch, an intimate link with other women who were gratefully buying up the product by the case. One printer who ran out of Lydia's picture for the labels substituted an old print of Queen Victoria. If anybody noticed the difference, there was certainly no decrease in sales.

In 1881 Lydia's two oldest boys died within weeks of each other, but by then the business had scores of people on the payroll. Lydia had more money than she had ever dreamed of, with sales approaching a million dollars a year. Then in 1883, she too passed away, from overwork, some people said.

As for Isaac Pinkham, the inspiration for it all, he was now out of the woods for good, all his old debts paid up in full. Free from the burden of work, he settled down to a long and ripe old age enjoying the profits of Lydia Pinkham's Vegetable Compound, "The Greatest Medical Discovery Since the Dawn of History."

Girl Bandit Goofed Badly

History of the feminist movement is replete with stories of women competing successfully with men in such fields as banking, law, the arts and science. But occasionally one can find an instance in which the lady was a failure.

For example, it is notable that the last stagecoach robber in the American West was a woman. Probably her greatest mistake was that she took up the profession after progress had already made it obsolete.

At age 17, Pearl Hart, student at a New England girls' boarding school, fell madly in love with an itinerant gambler who was stranded in town overnight when he missed his train. Together the pair ran off to Chicago to visit the great Colombian Exposition of 1893.

While Clarence worked at a midway card game, Pearl spent every minute at the Wild West show, admiring the dramatic performances of cowboys, cattle rustlers, desperadoes and lawmen. An impressionable girl, she listened intently to their every word and decided that her destiny lay in the West, in the midst of the glamorous life on the frontier.

When they reached Colorado, Clarence soon disappeared. Pearl supported herself by whatever work she could find, mining camp cook, hotel maid or saloon waitress. None of it was fun.

Moving around from job to job, Pearl presently drifted to Arizona where she became engaged to a prospector named Joe Boot. One day over beans and bacon, while Pearl was complaining about her hard life of drudgery and poverty, Joe suggested that they hold up the stagecoach. (Joe was not an intellectual giant.)

In 1899 stage routes still served some isolated communities in the West, but the transport of valuables such as gold and payrolls had long since been taken over by the railroads. There hadn't been a stage robbery in Arizona in years.

As preparation for their escapade, Pearl dressed in man's clothing, her hair tucked into a hat, but apart from that made no attempt at disguise. On the appointed afternoon they rode a few miles out from town, and as the stage rounded a bend, brandished pistols in the face of the startled driver. From the three frightened passengers, two traveling salesmen and a Chinese cook with a pigtail, Pearl collected nearly $400. Then in the grand tradition of the Old West she returned a single dollar to each victim for food and lodging.

Of course they were caught. The sheriff and his posse found the two bandits asleep in the shade of a tree less than a mile from the scene of the crime. When the tale was picked up by the telegraph, newspapers as far away as St. Louis carried stories of the Arizona Lady Bandit.

While awaiting trial, Pearl reveled in the publicity, and fed the fires by swallowing talcum powder in a phony suicide attempt, and by plotting an escape with the trusty who brought meals to her cell.

After weeks of fanfare the case came to trial in Yuma, with full press coverage and photographers jostling for a shot of the Lady Bandit of the West. By some miraculous circumstances — perhaps something to do with frontier chivalry — Pearl was acquitted by the jury, while poor Joe was found guilty and sentenced to 30 years. The chauvinist judge was furious with the jury.

Following her release Pearl faded quickly from the limelight. For a time she tried her hand at acting, and then toured with a carnival selling pictures of herself and Joe holding hands through the bars of adjacent jail cells. After she dropped completely from sight a rumor spread that she had married the foreman of the jury and had gone to join him in Utah in the unglamorous, but honest, profession of raising sheep. Someone else maintained years later that she was running a cigar store in Kansas City. Pearl and Joe made their own small contribution to the folklore of the West. They demonstrated too that the course of true love is never smooth, and that on some days it is impossible to win.

"Bluestocking" Lady Found Love

Her father wanted a boy for his first-born but quickly cast off his disappointment. Right from the beginning he concentrated on guiding his daughter's footsteps along the path of intellectual attainment, lavishing upon her the classical education he had planned for a son.

As a result of this early preparation, she became the first true female intellectual in awakening America — lecturer, author, linguist and philosopher. But the romantic relationships of life treasured by every woman seemed somehow to pass her by.

Margaret Fuller was born near Boston in 1810, daughter of a prominent politician, a man of considerable learning. By the time the child was six she was reading the classical Latin authors and was well advanced on the study of French, Greek and mathematics.

In attending the local school with other children, Margaret was not a good mixer. Playmates jeered at the big words she sometimes used, and her response to such teasing was usually a temper tantrum. Occasionally too she would indulge in periods of withdrawal during which she would neither eat nor speak for several days.

Beginning when she was about 16, a number of young men came across her path. Most were college students from Harvard or Yale, serious young gentlemen who enjoyed discussions with Margaret on such subjects as metaphysics and the new German philosophers. Strangely, however, each one drifted away in turn to seek the companionship of less scholarly young ladies.

By age 25 Margaret was resigned to facing life as an old maid, but by this time she had published a book on philosophy and was well known for her organized conversation sessions at which she sought to convince women that, as individuals they should try to realize their highest intellectual and spiritual potential. At about the same time she also won widespread acclaim for a magazine article, "The Great Lawsuit — Woman versus Man," which became a blueprint for the feminist movement — still a few years in the future.

While still well short of 30 Margaret was appointed editor of the most prestigious philosophical journal in New England, an unheard of position for a woman in those days. Here she soon attracted the attention of Horace Greeley, the famous New York editor who invited her to become his assistant. Thus Margaret Fuller became the first woman to hold an important place on any large newspaper.

In 1846, when she was a mature young woman of 35, Greeley sent her to Europe as special correspondent. Here from the great cities of the Old World she sent back graphic portrayals of social conditions as well as interviews with famous poets, writers and painters of the day. In Poland she met a great mystic who told her that for all her fame her life was empty. "You exist as a ghost that whispers about desires it is incapable of experiencing itself."

Six months later in Rome she discovered what this meant. In Saint Peter's Square she met a young Italian nobleman who swept her off her feet in a whirlwind courtship. Within three weeks they were married, secretly because of religious difference, and became the happy occupants of a small villa on the outskirts of Rome.

Now for the first time Margaret knew the meaning of happiness. Italy was then engaged in a war for independence from Austria, and as a journalist Margaret adapted readily to the role of war correspondent as her dispatches to New York sparkled with new warmth and humanity.

Presently she became pregnant, and her husband was at her side when their son was born in their honeymoon villa.

In due course the time arrived to go home again. In May 1850 Margaret with her husband and baby sailed for America. The ship never reached harbor. In a great storm off Fire Island the vessel broke in two and sank within sight of helpless watchers off the coast of New Jersey. Two days later the body of Margaret's baby washed ashore. Of Margaret herself or her husband, no sign was ever seen again.

This Queen Gave Up Her Throne

Poor Christina! She was born a princess in an illustrious royal family but grew up to be ugly, bad-tempered and a notorious liar. At age 18 she became a ruling queen in her own right but abandoned the job in disgust 10 years later and left the country.

Christina was born in Sweden in 1626, daughter of a great king Gustavus Adolphus. At an early age she was smitten by smallpox, which left her face badly scarred. In addition, one shoulder was deformed, causing it to rise higher than the other. No doubt these misfortunes had an influence on the character and personality of the young girl.

When Christina was six, her father was killed in battle, thus placing the child in line for the throne, and the following years were spent in preparation for the task of ruling the country. For this reason she was given an intensive man's education, as well as training in the masculine arts of horsemanship and dexterity in arms. Most of the time she wore male attire, and had little time for the interests usually associated with young girls.

Christina proved to be a brilliant student, amazing her teachers with her aptitude for statecraft, the arts, science and languages. At 14 she was already attending ministerial meetings on national affairs and at 18 ascended the throne as sole ruler of Sweden.

In spite of her bad temper, Christina proved to be a very good queen. She quickly ended a war with Germany that had dragged on for years. Next she ordered a stop to fighting among the noble families of Sweden. As a matter of royal policy, artists, musicians and writers were welcome visitors to the Swedish court.

Education, industry and foreign trade all prospered under her guidance. She was a pioneer in the philosophy of using government money to promote the interests of the people and the country as a whole. Because she was years ahead of her time, Christina was sometimes criticized for extravagance.

Then on her 27th birthday Christina astonished her subjects and the crowned heads of all Europe by announcing that she no longer wanted to be queen. When pressed for a reason she said that the burden of running the country was too much for a woman. Her real reason was altogether different. Most of all was the pressure on her from all sides to select a husband promptly so that she might produce an heir to the throne. Christina knew that she was not beautiful, but more than that she valued her independence. Christina did not want to be married.

Having made up her mind, the young queen issued a proclamation appointing a young second cousin to be king of Sweden in her place. In 1654 she packed her personal belongings and left the country for Rome.

Rome at that time was not only a great center of scholarship and art, but was also headquarters for a maze of European political intrigue. Christina entered actively into both of these worlds. But more than the plots among kings and princes, the former queen enjoyed her freedom to patronize the arts and music.

In her Roman palace, Christina assembled the world's greatest collection of paintings, sculptures and medallions. She founded an academy for the study of philosophy (which still stands) where the great men of letters and science gathered together. Upon her instigation, the first public opera house in Rome was opened, and she sponsored the work of numerous talented musicians.

Persistent whispers in the villas and meeting places of Rome linked Christina's name romantically with that of a gentleman prominent in public affairs and church politics. Letters between the two, discovered more than a hundred years later, seemed to confirm the belief that they shared a deeply touching and intimate relationship.

Christina left a great fortune in books and paintings to be enjoyed by future generations. She also bequeathed an example of womanly independence in that she gave up a royal throne rather than submit to bondage in a marriage of convenience.

Circus Actress Assumes Throne

As a young girl, Theodora lived a life of sin, indulging in casual relationships with a great many men. But the history of her time reveals how she eventually became a champion of true womanly virtue and the ruler of a great empire.

Theodora was born to a circus family at Constantinople (now Istanbul) in the year A.D. 500. Both of her parents were professional entertainers and eagerly trained the child for the stage as soon as she could toddle. Theodora performed at the Hippodrome, the great municipal stadium for public extravaganzas, before she was 10. Soon thereafter she received additional training in the arts of providing private entertainment for prominent gentlemen of the city. In those days this was regarded as a normal activity for talented and beautiful ladies of the theater.

In the middle of her teen years, Theodora set out on a grand tour with the circus, a prolonged journey which took the performers all across North Africa as far as Egypt. Theodora advanced in her profession, and in sharing the most private thoughts of eminent men, grew in wisdom beyond her years.

Upon returning to Constantinople, Theodora was 23. On her first reappearance at the Hippodrome, a man named Justinian, son of the emperor, was captivated by her beauty. Although Justinian was more than 20 years older than the girl, he begged her to give up the stage and marry him.

Many difficulties lay in the way. Because of Theodora's background in the theater and her style of life, it was necessary to obtain repeal of a law which prohibited gentlemen of the upper classes from marrying actresses. This law had been passed years earlier to protect impressionable young men of good families from designing women with eyes on their money. Justinian succeeded in having the law changed and the two were married. Very soon thereafter, Justinian's father died, and his son became emperor with his bride Theodora sharing the throne as his empress.

Justinian was not a very good ruler, being a weak, middle-aged man whose life had long been devoted to the gratification of sensual pleasures. Before very long the peace of the city was disrupted when two rival groups of chariot racers, the Blues and the Greens, created widespread disorder in violent rioting. Justinian became terrified, and feared that the rioters would attack him personally.

As fighting raged in the streets he prepared a ship in the harbor and urged Theodora to sail away with him to safety. Theodora refused to run away, and used all of her persuasive powers to encourage her weak husband to stand his ground. Reluctantly, Justinian agreed, and with Theodora's strong right hand to guide him, he soon found ways to end the rioting. Unfortunately Justinian did not recover from this confrontation with fear and died suddenly, even as peace returned to the city.

Now Theodora, former circus performer and courtesan, found herself faced with responsibilities few men could master. First she carefully selected wise men to serve as administrators, while she personally introduced a number of social reforms, particularly pertaining to women.

Theodora built public hospitals for girls and women of all ages and established homes for rehabilitation of prostitutes. Wisely, she did not prohibit prostitution nor did she place restrictions on the circus or theater. For some women in those days, the only alternative to prostitution was starvation or slavery. Instead, as these unfortunate women reached a time of life in which their skills or charms could no longer buy bread, they were trained in simple tasks essential in caring for others, tending to the sick and comforting the aged.

With equal wisdom, Theodora refrained from destroying the rowdy gangs of chariot racers. Under her firm control the two groups were encouraged to compete as ceremonial teams honoring the empress in her public appearances. When Theodora entered the Hippodrome or moved through the streets of the city, the rival chariot racers displayed their horsemanship and the intricacy of their wheeling maneuvers for the approval of their patroness and the applause of assembled citizens.

Following the death of her husband, Theodora adopted the new religion of Christianity, which then was spreading rapidly throughout the world. She ruled for more than 10 years, a remarkable woman who cared for the welfare of her people. Many of her social reforms endured for generations. The world was poorer when she passed away in the prime of life at age 48.

She Became Patron Saint of Farm Wives

One of the most inspiring women of the early Christian church was Bridget of Ireland, who eventually became the patron saint of farm wives everywhere in the British Isles.

Bridget was born about A.D. 450, daughter of a mountain tribal chief. When she was 13, Bridget was so fair of face and so enchanting of manner that her father decided to sell her to the high king of Ireland.

Accordingly, he drove her in his chariot to the king's castle and left her outside the walls while he went inside to make a bargain.

As Bridget waited with the horses, a crippled beggar approached asking for money or food. Having neither money nor food to offer, Bridget gave the beggar her father's sword, a noble weapon encrusted with precious stones.

When the king emerged from his castle to inspect what he had bought, he learned of her gift to the beggar and immediately turned his back, saying that he wanted nothing to do with so extravagant a female.

When Bridget and her angry father arrived back at their tribal home, the father renounced her as a daughter, casting her out of the family circle and assigning her to be one of the servants. The other servants took malicious pleasure in mistreating the girl who had once been their mistress. When she was awkward at milking the cows or churning the butter, they denied her a share of food at mealtime. But Bridget was a Christian girl and found consolation and strength in her religion.

When she was 17, Bridget's father attempted to sell her once more, this time to a secondary nobleman. But Bridget heard of the transaction and fled deep into the forest. Under shelter of a great oak tree she built for herself a small hut of branches and clay from the riverbank. This humble dwelling became in time the hub of a community of Christian women who devoted their lives to good works and prayer, and to spreading the word of God.

In spite of opposition and insult from pagan men in the surrounding countryside, Bridget's small community of women endured to become the first religious sisterhood in all Ireland.

In the hard work of maintaining their own independence, Bridget and her sisters became expert in the arts of life and shared their knowledge freely with farm wives anywhere within a day's walk.

If a cow was ready to give birth, or if a sickness was afflicting a fowl, one of the sisters was certain to appear to offer help. They cared for the sick and helped with the work in any family crisis. They encouraged the hens to lay and churned milk until great golden blobs of butter appeared, then disposing of the buttermilk to grateful pigs in the sty. Bridget and her sisters asked nothing for their work, but quietly spoke only of the word of God and the hope for salvation.

Such Christian charity and faith in God became known to all Ireland, as women spread the word from one house to another. The name of Bridget today is commemorated in churches, convents, orphanages and hospitals all over the Christian world.

Of the scores of legends surrounding her life, one story maintains that Bridget was the reincarnation of Saint Patrick who died about the year she was born. Her lifetime of work as an evangelist completed the task undertaken by Patrick of converting Ireland from paganism to Christianity.

When Bridget died at 71, a remarkable age for a woman in those times, she was buried at first under the oak tree where years earlier she had found refuge after escaping from her cruel father. The gravesite is still honored as a shrine at which hundreds of pilgrims pray each year.

Later the body was removed to Downpatrick and placed beside the grave of the greatest Christian missionary in Irish history, Saint Patrick himself, the liberated slave who first brought the teachings of Christ to pagan Ireland.

Mercy Missions End in Mysterious Deaths

Celeste Brinville grew up in Paris about 1650, a time when the upper classes of the city devoted their entire lives to the pursuit of pleasure. The lively young girl longed to take part in the costume balls and gala parties at the great fashionable houses.

But her father, a magistrate, was very strict and kept his only daughter under close control. A young girl, the father believed, should be occupied only with her prayers and with doing good deeds for others.

By the time she was 21, Celeste hated her father. She felt that he was an unreasonable and stubborn obstacle to her happiness. Night after night in her bedchamber she dreamed of finding some way out of the difficulty that was choking her young life.

Finally after a great deal of thought, Celeste turned her feminine charms on a shy young chemist at a shop in the neighborhood. She tempted him, promising him the gift of virginal love, if he would provide her with a supply of poison. At first the young man was unsure; he knew very little about poisons. But the reward Celeste offered by far outweighed all other considerations, and the young chemist agreed to do his best.

When the first potion was secretly delivered by the hand of the chemist, Celeste administered it to her maid in a glass of wine. However to her dismay, the stupid girl suffered only a stomach ache and a brief fainting spell. Clearly the poison would have to be stronger. Reaffirming her promise to him with downcast eyes, Celeste urged the young man to renewed efforts in concocting something stronger.

Soon thereafter, Celeste began a schedule of regular visits to the city hospitals. She chatted cheerfully with the patients and distributed small sweet cakes, made with her own hands, as a special treat. Her father praised her for this noble work of charity, and the nurses at the hospitals admired Celeste as a saint. They noted that the young visitor wept in sadness when her favorite patients weakened and died.

About the same time, Celeste's father became ill of a mysterious stomach ailment. In great concern, Celeste dismissed the old family cook and personally assumed the task of feeding her failing father. But alas, the good magistrate soon died, not in the peace of a happy death, but in the agony of a stomach eaten away by poison.

At the funeral everyone pointed to Celeste as a model daughter, a model of obedience and charity. But even then the hand of fate was in motion.

On the day of the magistrate's death, the young chemist, more and more eager to reap his reward, was industriously concocting a new and deadly poison in his laboratory. As his fingers added the final ingredient, a terrific explosion took place, destroying the young man and his equipment.

Celeste's guilty secret might yet have been safe, but the authorities found in the young man's apartment passionate letters to the girl he hoped to win, as well as detailed descriptions of the work in blending poisons for her.

Celeste was arrested and placed in the dread prison, the Bastille, while the magistrates of the city deliberated. They considered questioning her under torture, and she spent some days in the torture chamber awaiting their decision. After a time the magistrates agreed that Celeste was guilty of murder and sentenced her to death. When this was communicated to her, Celeste shrugged indifferently and offered to confess all.

Because of the monstrous nature of her many crimes, the magistrates determined that the young girl must be possessed by an evil spirit. In this case her execution must follow a prescribed ritual so as to destroy the evil spirit as well as the human body which housed it.

On a chill morning in the courtyard of the grim prison, Celeste went to her death for the murder of a score of persons. First the executioner with swift professional skill and a single blow separated the head from the body. Then a group of surgeons dissected the torso, following a strict procedure established for such cases. Then the remains were placed in a furnace, and witnesses observed until all was consumed.

As a final act of vengeance, an official finally stepped on a platform and read a proclamation saying that the name of Celeste

Brinville must not be spoken by any citizen of Paris for at least a hundred years. So ends the story of a girl who was impatient to grow up, and whose impatience turned out to be her undoing.

Nameless Waif Attains Notable Niche in History

On Saint Catherine's Day, November 25, 1864, in the country of Livonia, an elderly priest was returning home at dusk when his horse shied in fright at a dark mound in the snow. Dismounting to investigate, the pastor found an infant girl wrapped only in a single thin blanket. When he recovered from his astonishment, the priest folded his cloak carefully around the babe and hurried home to the cottage where his sister was keeping supper warm on the stove.

Since there was no identification of any kind with the beautiful dark-eyed child, the pastor and his sister accepted her as a gift from God. Here in a small Livonian village with her foster parents, Catherine grew into a tall enchanting maiden with a sweet voice and a happy disposition. Of course she knew nothing of her past, but she loved the old priest as if he were her own father.

In 1702, when Catherine was 18, a great army from nearby Russia invaded Livonia, intent on conquering the small country. Around the village where Catherine and her foster parents lived, the fighting was very fierce. By nightfall, dead and wounded men of both sides were shouting: this beautiful Livonian jewel will be a prize for our general. It is well known he has a taste for warm-blooded young girls.

Dragged forcibly to the general's tent, Catherine fell on her knees before the bearded ferocious Russian. In tears she begged permission to search the battlefield for her beloved foster father, now missing since he went to minister to the wounded. When the general hesitated, a very tall officer at his side offered to accompany the girl.

After searching well into the hours of night, the two finally found the old man, wounded, but alive. The tall young officer ordered two Russian soldiers to carry the priest to his cottage. Then he turned sternly to Catherine. You must now escape while you can, he told her, pressing a purse of gold money into her hand. But no; Catherine refused. She had pledged the general to return to captivity if only she could save her foster father. Now she was ready to pay the required price — her virtue, her honor, even her life.

Once more in the Russian camp, the tall officer told the general of their search. Then with a laugh he asked the older man: what price will you take for your captive Livonian jewel? The general laughed in turn and added a few words in gutteral Russian.

Catherine was led away to another tent, even more ornate and luxurious than that of the general. Soon the girl learned the identity of the tall officer. She had been purchased as a trophy by Peter the Great, Emperor of Russia.

Thus Catherine the orphan waif became the servant and companion of a great ruler and military leader. Before long he came to value her advice, spoken softly in his ear at the end of each day. She accompanied him on his great military campaigns, and only Catherine with her soft voice and gentle fingertips had the power to ease the terrible headaches from which the dynamic emperor suffered. As the two grew closer, they shared the task of devising great plans for Russia.

Then in 1711, Peter the Great suffered a serious military defeat. His army in a war against the Turks became surrounded by the enemy. Peter himself was in danger of being taken prisoner by enemies who had reason to hate him. But at this point, Catherine, using her growing influence in secret diplomacy, privately negotiated with the Turks for a compromise treaty. Peter and his army were permitted to leave Turkey in honorable withdrawal and peace between the two countries was established at least for a time.

Safely back home in Russia, Peter made Catherine his bride, to share his throne as empress — just 10 years after her capture as prisoner in the village in Livonia.

In the years that followed, Peter the Great continued to work like the giant he was at great accomplishments in war and peace. His terrible headaches grew steadily worse, and the emperor depended more and more heavily on Catherine. Peter died in 1725, and his wife, the nameless waif found in a snowdrift in Livonia, assumed the throne as Catherine I, Empress of Russia. Unfortunately, her role as monarch was brief. Catherine I was empress of all Russia only from 1725 until her death in 1727.

FOOTNOTES TO HISTORY

Consisting of Fragments
Frequently Ignored
by Serious
Scholars

Women in Combat a Matter of Historical Record

Opponents of the Equal Rights Amendment consistently attempt to make an issue of the horrifying possibility that women could be drafted for combat service with the armed forces. While this prospect is highly unlikely, many people find it difficult to get upset about the point even in theory. Military history is liberally sprinkled with stories about the hair-raising adventures of women who became combat soldiers by choice.

There was Kit Cavanagh, for example, who donned male attire and joined the British army in 1693 in search of the husband who had deserted her. Someone said at the time that Kit had about as much sex appeal as a problem in mathematics, a circumstance which may have had something to do with her husband's departure.

In the war between England and France this lady warrior served with the Royal Dragoons at battles in Holland, Belgium, France and Germany. When she was finally wounded in the head, the surgeons discovered her sex and she was reassigned as a cook in the officers mess, wearing a conventional feminine dress. Here at the end of a search lasting 11 years she was reunited with her wandering husband.

Another English lady in search of a lost husband was Ann Mills who joined the British Marines as a man about 1740. During a landing on the coast of France she was wounded in the leg and in the lower abdomen. Fearful that the surgeons would discover her secret, she did not disclose the latter wound, but removed the bullet herself despite terrible pain.

There is no record if she ever found her husband, but someone who served with her made a drawing of the lady marine in action. She is shown with upraised sword in one hand and the dripping head of a Frenchman in the other.

Probably the first organized women's combat army in modern history was formed by the king of Dahomey in West Africa about 1850. When a British explorer visited the country about 1863, he was not impressed by what he saw of the lady troops in training.

"Most of them," he wrote in his journal, "are hideously ugly, and they maneuver with the precision of a flock of sheep." In derision the Englishman further observed. "The officers undoubtedly are selected for the size of their posteriors."

But the snooty Englishman was speaking strictly from ignorance. The fighting women of Dahomey comprised a serious military unit which protected that peaceful country against marauding neighbors. When it was necessary for the ladies to attack invaders, they moved barefoot in absolute silence through brush and jungle. Their weapons were long knives and short spears, and their strategy was to fall on the enemy by surprise in the gray half-light of dawn.

No elite military unit was ever held in higher esteem; every member of the 2,500-women force was a wife of the king. But male chauvinism eventually came into play. The women's army of Dahomey was disbanded by the French in 1892 when the little country became a French colony.

Other women's fighting groups in the early 20th century included a band of Turkish riflewomen whose sniping terrorized the British at Gallipoli in 1915. In the same war and a bit to the north, the Russians had a female fighting unit known as the Battalion of Death.

Several countries of Europe and the New World have produced their own militant women who donned uniforms and fought in the ranks beside their men. Every war seems to inspire at least a few, and there is no way of knowing how many may serve without detection. However it is safe to say that the proficiency of women in combat has nothing to do with their sex or the size of their posteriors.

A Colony Founded on Greed Perished

Everybody knows that Christopher Columbus discovered the New World when he sighted the coast of San Salvador in October 1492. Not so well known is the tale of the colony he established on the island of Haiti and the fate of the 39 Spanish settlers.

For several weeks after the first historic sighting of land, the little Spanish fleet of three ships loitered among the islands of the Caribbean, admiring the scenery and keeping a lookout for signs of gold or other treasure. The *Pinta* became separated from the other two vessels, and on December 24 the *Santa Maria* and the *Nina* floated idly in fine weather off the north coast of Haiti. It was a beautiful moonlight night, with the sea as smooth as milk in a bowl. Perhaps the sailors were a bit careless on this Christmas Eve so far from home, but presently the *Santa Maria* drifted aground on a sandbar near the beach.

Frantically through the night, all hands toiled to dislodge the trapped vessel but to no avail. At dawn the caravelle was resting on her side on the bar with the gentle waters of the tide splashing over the exposed keel. Before long a canoe bearing a naked savage set out from shore. By sign language the Indian conveyed that he was a messenger from the local king bringing an offer of help. As a token of friendship he presented Columbus with a beautifully carved gold mask, a gesture which impressed the Spaniard profoundly. But in spite of the efforts of 20 canoes manned by half a hundred muscular Indians, the *Santa Maria* refused to budge from her sandy bed. Columbus now was in a difficult predicament. How would he explain the loss of his ship? When a second gift from the king arrived — this time in the form of an intricably carved gold belt — his sense of despair lightened appreciably.

Obviously it would seem that gold treasure was abundant on the island, and at this point the admiral decided to establish a settlement on the spot — the first colony in the New World — while he would return to Spain with his report for the king and queen. Accordingly, the *Santa Maria* was dismantled where she lay and her timbers were used to build a stout stockade on shore. The 39 men comprising the ship's crew were then designated settlers and put ashore with all available supplies. Columbus called the colony La Navidad, or Nativity, because the landing took place on Christmas Day.

Before sailing away on the *Nina* Columbus delivered an inspiring farewell address. He directed the settlers to gather all the gold or other treasure they could find for the glory of Spain. As for their personal conduct, he enjoined them particularly not to become involved with the native Indian women.

Upon arriving in Spain, Columbus received a regal welcome, and the king and queen proved to be generous in providing ships and funds for a second expedition. So after an absence of 11 months almost to the day, Columbus once more found himself within sight of the coast of Haiti in November 1493. He was surprised, as the fleet approached the coast, that none of his colonists appeared on the beach to wave a welcome. A landing party going ashore found two dead bodies near the bank of a stream. It was impossible to tell if they were Indians or Europeans, but one had a knotted rope around his neck and the other had his ankles bound together. When a third corpse was found with a thick black beard, Columbus began to suspect that something had gone seriously wrong.

Cruising slowly along the coast, the Spaniards finally found the bay where the *Santa Maria* had foundered and the site of the colony La Navidad. Nothing remained of the stockade fashioned from stout ship's timbers but a small pile of charred rubble. No sign of life could be found. Under questioning by the angry Spaniards, the Indians blandly told conflicting tales. Some of the settlers, they said, died of illness. Others fought among themselves, with fatal results. Tales were told of raids by unfriendly tribes from other parts of the island. One consistent thread of truth emerged. Every one of the Spanish sailors — enjoined to celibacy by their leader — had taken for himself at least three, and in some cases four or five, young women from the Indian villages.

For their sins they forfeited their lives, some of them suddenly as they walked in the shade of a forest pathway, others more painfully under the slow avenging knives of outraged fathers or husbands.

How the Puritans Cheated Charles II of Revenge

In 1649 a Puritan revolutionary court in England condemned the reigning monarch King Charles to death. The sentence was carried out by chopping off the king's head before a cheering crowd. As it happened, however, the revolutionary Puritan regime in Britain lasted only for 11 years. In 1660 another King Charles was seated on the throne, thoroughly determined to avenge the murder of his father. Scores of prominent Puritans were rounded up. Some were hanged; others were cast into dungeons to starve. Only a handful of the leaders escaped. Two of the officers who had signed the king's death warrant managed under false names to board a ship bound for the Puritan colony in America. They were Edward Whalley and his son-in-law William Goffe.

On July 27, 1660, their ship arrived at Boston in the Massachusetts Bay Colony. Perhaps foolishly, the two men made no secret of their true identity, but even boasted to American Puritans of their role in the rebellion and the death of the king. They were welcomed by Governor John Endicott and were entertained by the Rev. Charles Chauncey, Harvard College president. Not surprisingly, news of the presence of these two fugitive Puritans in Boston soon got back to King Charles in England. In November a special royal messenger arrived in the colony bearing a warrant for the apprehension of Whalley and Goffe, dead or alive.

Colonial authorities made no immediate move to carry out the arrest, but learning of their danger the two men made their way through a winter wilderness to the New Haven Colony, 160 miles away. Here again, sympathetic Puritans extended wholehearted hospitality. Infuriated by the failure of colonial powers to arrest the fugitives, King Charles next sent out a military expedition to hunt down the two men. In 1664 scores of British soldiers scoured the countryside around New Haven, while their quarry moved by night from one hiding place to the next. They finally found refuge at the home of the Rev. John Russell in the village of Hadley. Here the regicides were hidden in a large underground room that could be reached only through a trapdoor. This room became home for the hunted men for 10 years. The pastor with the help of his wife and two children cared for their every need. Over the years the good clergyman and his family were themselves prisoners in a way. They dared not leave the house unattended; one person had to remain constantly on guard.

Meanwhile back in England, Frances Goffe faithfully wrote letters to her husband and father. This secret correspondence was dependent on the cooperation of the famous Puritan clergyman Increase Mather of Boston who served as intermediary. In a letter dated August 1674, Goffe wrote Frances that her father was dead and was buried under the floor of the cellar where he had spent his declining years. Then in 1675 the entire Connecticut Valley was ravaged by war, as bands of Indians swept through the country, plundering and burning everything in their path. In the ferocity of this turmoil, the exchange of correspondence between the hunted man and his wife in England came to an end. A final letter was written by Goffe in 1679 — nearly 20 years after his escape from England — in which he deplored the infirmities of old age and the terrible curse of loneliness. Nothing more is known of his fate, not when he died nor where he lies buried.

The people of New Haven did not completely forget their unfortunate guests, even as time passed and one generation gave way to the next. As evidence of their Puritan heritage, citizens of New Haven can today point to two streets in their city bearing the names of Whalley and Goffe. In fleeing from their homeland to escape the king's rage, they sacrificed the good things of normal life, but they cheated King Charles of at least a part of his vengeance.

How Women Won the Right to Vote

When the first blush of dawn arose on the 20th century, the women's crusade for the right to vote seemed to have reached a solid dead end.

Susan B. Anthony and Elizabeth Cady Stanton, the two pioneer leaders who had carried the burden for 50 years, were old and exhausted. Irregular meetings were still held at which indifferent audiences dozed to the sound of tired speeches. As someone said at the ime, the women's movement was like a broken record aimlessly repeating empty sounds over and over.

In 1907 Elizabeth Stanton's daughter Harriot came home from England with exciting news about the suffragist movement in London. Under the vigorous leadership of Emmaline Pankhurst and her two daughters, British feminists had learned how to pelt policemen with rocks, how to kick and scratch when arrested, and how to use the hatpin and the umbrella as weapons of self-defense.

Inspired by the vitality of the movement in Britain, a new generation of leaders emerged on the scene in America. One of these was Carrie Chapman Catt, a dignified lady, orderly, efficient, methodical. She organized parades and processions and spoke at political gatherings and conventions.

A different soul entirely was Alice Paul, an electric type, the lady who put fire and brimstone into the women's movement. Having tasted the blood of battle with the Pankhurst ladies in London, Alice organized a great army of militant women with colorful costumes and plenty of dash.

They wore purple, white, and gold — the colors of the movement — and their public demonstrations were designed for maximum impact. Picketing the White House, the Capitol, and other public buildings, these new crusaders for the right to vote fought with police who attempted to interfere. Arrests became common. Hundreds were literally dragged off to jail, their skirts trailing in the gutters.

Alice Paul and others endured hunger strikes; in some cases they were forcibly fed. One officious prosecutor tried to have Alice certified insane, without success.

As national interest in the movement was revitalized, Alice organized the Congressional Union, a special elite group dedicated to disturbing the peace and inertia of politicians as much as possible. The picket line around the White House, set up in January 1917, never faltered for a year and a half, as 1,000 women took their turns at walking a tour on the line. Finally in the Congressional election campaign of 1918, both major political parties came out in favor of the right to vote for women.

And that is the way the battle was won. On May 21, 1919, the House of Representatives passed the 19th amendment to the Constitution by the comfortable vote of 304 to 90; the Senate followed with a tally of 66 to 30. A year later in the summer of 1920, ratification of the amendment by two-thirds of the states was officially proclaimed, and the vote for women became the law of the land. The long hard fight was over.

Adams Ignored Wife's Advice

In the early days of the American Revolution, Mrs. Abigail Adams of Massachusetts sent a letter to her husband John, the man who would later become the nation's first vice president and the second president.

But in 1775 John Adams was in Philadelphia serving with the Continental Congress, while Abigail was back home in Massachusetts tending to the children and the family farm, at the same time keeping an eye out for marauding Redcoats.

In this famous letter to her husband, Abigail said in effect: John, when you are drawing up plans for a new democratic United States, where everybody is free and equal, remember the ladies. Well, as the history books show, the Continental Congress did not remember the ladies by making them equal, and according to legend, John Adams could not believe that his wife was serious in what she said.

More than 145 years passed between Abigail's letter to her husband and final passage of a law giving women the right to vote in 1920. Judging by what is known of Abigail's character, it is almost certain that she never let John forget his mistake.

Modern Feminists Owe Debt to Pioneers

In spite of some last-ditch holding actions by diehard reactionary males, the war between the sexes in the United States is virtually over. The men, traditional masters of the world for centuries, suffered a decisive defeat this year (1975) when the National Soap Box Derby was won by a contestant of the opposite sex. The psychological impact of this catastrophe was second only to that suffered on the playing fields of the country when Little League baseball was stripped of its exclusive masculinity.

An index of the scope of seven-league accomplishments by the feminist movement can be found in the national elections of 1974. In addition to 18 females winning seats in the House of Representatives, more than 600 were elected to state and local office. There are now seven women's professional football teams drawing good crowds of spectators across the country. The churches are busily ordaining feminine clergypersons, while business and the professions are being infiltrated steadily and progressively.

Altogether it can be said that the feminist movement is perfumed with the sweet smell of success. But today, in the last phases of Armageddon, the unbiased observer cannot escape the impression that contemporary feminist leadership lacks the monumental stature of the pioneers who launched the crusade for equality beginning about a hundred and fifty years ago. None of those early feminist agitators was noted for physical strength; some indeed were diminutive; but the girls who reap the harvest of their toil today owe these ancestral warriors a debt of gratitude beyond measure.

In 1848, following the first Women's Rights Convention at Seneca Falls, N.Y., Lucretia Mott and Elizabeth Cady Stanton issued a Declaration of Sentiment including the radical proposition that "all men and women are created equal." This astounding attack on the established order created more of a furore than the Communist Manifesto which was issued in the same year.

As the movement spread, its unpopularity increased. In 1853 Harpers Magazine denounced feminism as radical and heathen, going on to say that it was clearly anti-biblical. But the ladies persevered. In 1870, Susan B. Anthony, the George Washington of the crusade, was arrested and convicted of trying to vote in an election at Rochester. She refused to pay the fine, but no gentleman had the courage to send her to jail.

More than 50 years ahead of her time, Lucy Stone proposed that married women retain their maiden names. Amelia Bloomer shed her whalebone corset and invented a very practical trouser-like garment for which the world of fashion was not yet ready. When Carrie Chapman married George Catt in 1890, she insisted on a marriage contract providing for a four-month furlough each year, the free time to be devoted to the cause of women's rights.

Others were even more colorful. Victoria Woodhull, an eloquent and vigorous spokeswoman, attempted to dramatize the cause by running for President. However, her political views attracted less attention than her advocacy of free love. This too was part of her campaign platform. In the absence of any organized voting strength or sympathetic support from the press, these diligent activists relied almost entirely on the power of the female tongue, which, as Washington Irving once observed, is the only edged tool that grows keener by constant use.

Following the turn of the century, Anna Howard Shaw and Alice Paul organized protest marches in Washington and placed pickets around the White House. The great strategic victory came in 1919 when, in spite of bitter opposition in the Senate, Congress passed the Nineteenth Amendment giving women the right to vote. Stubborn male chauvinists still insist that wartime hysteria was a factor in passage of the amendment. Others point to the factor that hundreds of thousands of men were still overseas in France following the defeat of Germany. Be that as it may, the critical corner was turned.

One would like to think that in Valhalla, the special heaven for old soldiers, there is a place of honor set aside for these courageous warriors who fought the good fight in the face of ridicule, insult, and even scorn from groups and factions of their own sex. However, it is likely that the ladies would reject any suggestion of special privilege even in the hereafter. Special privilege was the issue to which they devoted their lives, and its destruction is the substance of their reward. One can see in mind's eye the old fires of indignation flicker once more into flame as a chorus of feminine harmony sings out: "Let there be Equal Rights and Equal Privilege. Let there be no Discrimination by Sex, be it in Heaven or be it in Hades."

As the war between the sexes tapers down to its final conclusion, perhaps the ladies who savor the heady taste of victory will have the grace to remember their predecessors with a small salute from the heart, as a gesture of thanks to those who made the whole thing possible.

A Blighted Romance Lost an Empire

In 1805 a Russian nobleman proposed marriage to a 15-year-old Spanish senorita. If the wedding had taken place, California today might be a Russian colony instead of an American state.

When Thomas Jefferson was President of the United States, Russia already had two settlements in North America, both in Alaska at Kodiak and Sitka. With an eye to extending his overseas possessions, Czar Alexander I of Russia sent his good friend Baron Nikolai Rezanov on a mission to promote and expand the American colonies.

A handsome widower of 42, Rezanov was an ambitious man who dreamed of one day making the entire west coast of North America a part of the Russian Empire. As a first step toward this goal, he outfitted a ship in Sitka and set sail southward to establish trade relations with the Spanish settlements in California.

Upon dropping anchor at San Francisco the Russians were greeted with gracious hospitality by the Spanish governor and his military commandant. Days of picnics, hunting parties and lavish dinners followed, but the Spaniards, on orders from higher headquarters in Mexico City, were cool to the idea of trade. Rezanov persisted in his effort, staging elegant parties aboard his ship and paying courtly attention to Dona Concepcion Arguello, beautiful young daughter of the military commandant. As the Russian showered the girl with gifts, he regaled her with moonlight tales of glamorous life at the royal Russian court of Saint Petersburg.

Very soon he proposed, and Concepcion accepted, but her parents disapproved. They were concerned not only about the difference in age and nationality but particularly about the difference in religion. However, the betrothed couple insisted that they were irrevocably in love. Rezanov, persuasive as always, spoke openly of an alliance between the two great empires of Russia and Spain that would be fostered by the marriage.

Finally the parents consented on condition that the union be approved by the Russian royal court in Saint Petersburg, by the Spanish royal court in Madrid and by the Vatican in Rome. With these three endorsements, the grand alliance of two empires seemed certain of realization. Rezanov was to return to Russia to obtain the necessary permissions there.

Following a brief stopover at Sitka, Rezanov sailed for home, arriving at Okhotsk on the east coast of Siberia in September. From here he set out on the 5,000-mile journey over frozen wasteland to Saint Petersburg. Illness interrupted his travels for a time, but he pressed on. In his weakened condition he fell from his horse at Krasnoyarsk while still far from his destination. Within an hour he was dead!

Back in Spanish California, Concepcion waited in vain for her lover. As time passed she rejected other offers of marriage but devoted her life to charity and nursing children of Indian villages. In 1842, 36 years after their final embrace, Concepcion learned of her lover's fate from an English fur trader. Immediately she entered a convent and spent the remainder of her days there.

Other attempts to establish Russian colonies in California followed, but none of them met with permanent success. The Russian dream of a great empire on the North American continent came to an end when the Baron Rezanov toppled from his horse in Siberia to strike his head.

Casket Girls Created a Unique Culture

Much of the rich culinary tradition associated with New Orleans and the Gulf Coast can be traced to the hard work and ingenuity of the Casket Girls, young ladies from France who came to the New World in the early 18th century in search of husbands.

Sponsored by the Bishop of Paris and chaperoned by a small group of nuns on every ship, the parties of hopeful maids arrived in New France during the two decades from 1700 to 1720. In age, some were as young as 13 or 14, and each girl was accompanied by a small casket containing a simple wedding dress and a few personal treasures such as hair ribbons or other trinkets.

All shared the determination to make some man very happy.

Although the men of the colony were properly enthusiastic about their arrival, the Casket Girls soon learned to their dismay that the culinary skills so painstakingly acquired in France were useless in the wild country of the colony. The plump chickens and fat little pigs of their native France were unknown. Even the fish in the sea were different, and in the marshes and bayous frightening, unfamiliar creatures lurked just under the surface of the water.

According to legend, a few of the girls rebelled against the barbaric staple diet of cornbread and boiled squirrel, and a handful of these returned to France.

For the most part, however, the Casket Girls got busy on the task of "make-do." Although such traditional French delicacies as smoked eel and truffles were memories of the past, the ladies quickly discovered the merits of wild turkeys and ducks, frogs with giant legs, possums, and turtles — all of which found their way into the great black iron stew pots.

Even more important, these enterprising cooks soon savored the delicate flavors of crawfish, pompano, and other aquatic species unknown to the people of Europe. From here it was just a step to find that the traditional fish soup of France, bouillabaisse, could be glorified by the addition of shrimp and oysters.

With the passage of time, as ham and chicken presently became more plentiful, morsels of these too were added to the pot. Thus was the foundation laid for jambalaya, a famous concoction composed of rice, shrimp, oysters, crab, tomatoes, chicken, ham and spices.

From the Indians, the Casket Girls learned the art of grinding up sassafras leaves to produce file, the magic ingredient of gumbo, a succulent spicy soup in which the creativity of the cook is given generous latitude.

Some of the passenger lists from the ships carrying the Casket Girls survive to the present day, carefully guarded against the destructive effects of time.

Records of their marriages are also, of course, carefully preserved for posterity. Numbers of the maids were married right on the beach, their feet still wet from the surf as they waded ashore to face a new life in a New World.

One account described how 70 couples were joined together in a single hilltop ceremony under the benevolent watchful eyes of the Parisian nuns.

Today the offspring of the Casket Girls can be found among the first families of New Orleans, Baton Rouge, Mobile, and other communities ranged along the coast near the mouth of the Mississippi.

An Ally Plotted to Undermine George Washington

Historians give General George Washington full credit for military victory in the Revolutionary War. Not so well known is the fact that Washington also had a powerful enemy in his own ranks — a man who plotted and schemed to ruin the commander in chief. Charles Lee has been described as a man consumed with pride and ambition, brilliant and scholarly but at the same time devious, ruthless and cunning. A former officer in the British army, Lee came to America in 1773 and soon met all the men who would assume importance in the Revolution. As the break with England approached, some members of the Continental Congress felt that Lee was the ideal man to lead the American army in the war with Britain. But sentiment in favor of a native-born American prevailed, and the appointment went to George Washington of Virginia.

The blow to Lee's ego was stupendous. He accepted a commission as major general under Washington, but as the war proceeded he consistently maneuvered to discredit his superior commander. Things went badly for the Americans at first, and Lee kept up a barrage of letters to Congress and to other officers on Washington's staff condemning the "fatal indecision" of the commander in chief. In the winter of 1776, as he moved his troops slowly across New Jersey to join Washington, Lee decided to spend the night of December 12 in a warm tavern instead of in camp with his men a few miles away. This proved to be a grievous mistake. A British patrol, seeking shelter from the cold, stumbled into the tavern next morning and triumphantly captured the biggest prisoner of the war. Some said that the loss of Lee would end the American rebellion.

The British held him for two years, during which time Lee, as a former British officer, feared for his life. To save his skin he offered his captors an elaborate plan for bringing an end to the revolt in the colonies. Finally in an exchange of prisoners Lee was returned to American lines and immediately resumed his efforts to displace Washington as commander in chief.

At the Battle of Monmouth the next year, Lee again attempted a daring act of treachery. Leading the Continental division under his command into a confused and tortuous maneuver, Lee finally ordered his troops to retreat from the field leaving Washington's group to face the British without support. For this violation Lee was tried by a military court. A lesser officer might have been shot for disobedience and cowardice under fire, but the sentence called only for a year's suspension. But the brilliant, merciless pen of this incredible egomaniac kept on with the devilish work. Lee's letters to Congress continued to denounce Washington as a "puffed up charlatan," while other American officers were described as useless incompetents. When the poison of his vituperation turned on the members of Congress themselves — a motley herd of bunglers, said Lee — a final decision was at last reached. Lee was dismissed from the army. When he died at Philadelphia in 1782 he was still fulminating against Washington.

Years later it was revealed that in 1776, when many Americans were seriously questioning Washington's military capability, Congress was at the point of replacing him with Lee as commander in chief. Only Lee's capture by the British prevented the change from taking place.

Historians still speculate on what might have been the consequences for America. For Lee was consistently scornful of Washington's respect for the authority of the Congress; he had no use whatever for the principle of military subservience to civilian government. The capture of this power hungry egocentric, followed by his dismissal from the army, was the luckiest possible break for the new American nation.

Businessman Answers Unique Knock of Opportunity

In 1849 hundreds of Americans headed west, drawn by the lure of the goldfields of California. Newspapers of the day were filled with accounts of fabulous wealth being scooped up from creek banks and ditches. Gold nuggets lay on the banks of streams waiting to be picked up by the sons of destiny. Paupers became millionaires overnight, and news accounts in the East fanned the flame of enthusiasm to a fever pitch.

Among those answering the call of opportunity was the younger son of a New York merchant family, 20-year-old Levi Strauss. With a stake consisting of bolts of cloth and rolls of canvas provided by his family, the young man set out to find fame and fortune in California. He made the journey by clipper ship around Cape Horn at the tip of South America, a rough and uncomfortable voyage of 17,000 miles. By the time young Strauss landed at San Francisco five months later, he had sold his entire supply of cloth to fellow passengers at premium prices. All he had left were some rolls of canvas which he hoped to sell to makers of covered wagons. But fate stepped in to change his plans.

Once on shore with his stock of canvas, young Levi was soon told by a new acquaintance that he had brought the wrong kind of merchandise. What was most in demand among the prospectors was sturdy clothing, and particularly pants that would stand up to the roughest usage. Inspired with the germ of an idea, Strauss sought out a tailor and presenting a roll of canvas asked him to make a pair of trousers for his friend. At first the tailor was dubious, but the price was right and he finally agreed. Canvas it would be! In appearance the resulting garment was less than elegant, but there was no question about the durability.

Within days young Levi Strauss was besieged by miners and wagon masters demanding to buy the new canvas pants. Levi sent a hurry-up message to his brothers back east for more canvas as quickly as possible. In the next few years, business expanded rapidly, spreading out from San Francisco all through the West. Tailors and seamstresses were recruited wherever they could be found. The two Strauss brothers came out from New York to help as the canvas pants became standard wear in the goldfields and cattle ranches. But sturdy as they were, the canvas pants were not indestructible. Prospectors had a habit of carrying gold nuggets around in their pockets for days on end, and the pockets thus became the first point to show wear. One old fellow named Alkali Ike brought his pants back to a tailor in Virginia City, Nevada, with a complaint about the pockets. Since the old fellow had first paid a visit to the corner saloon, his language was both eloquent and abusive. Rightfully angered in turn by his crusty customer, the tailor made the necessary repairs and then slipped across the street to the harness shop where he reinforced his stitches with copper rivets. That should fix the old goat!

Alkali Ike was delighted and offered to set up drinks for everybody in sight. From this incident the idea of copper rivets became the greatest breakthrough since the invention of canvas breeches. Levi Strauss invited the enterprising tailor to become a partner in the family business, and they obtained a patent on the rivet-reinforced canvas pants in 1873. When his patent expired in 1906, a dozen competing companies rushed to adopt the process. All of which goes to prove that hard work and good management are essential to success in business, but a little bit of luck and some human ingenuity can go a long way to help.

This Hero Was Rescued from Oblivion

Removal of a dead person from his assigned resting place is a radical and disagreeable undertaking, but compelling circumstances are occasionally unavoidable. Since the general topic happens to be of local interest at the moment, some history buff is bound to recall the saga of John Paul Jones, American naval hero whose body was exhumed more than a century after his death.

Every schoolboy has read of the famous Jones cry of defiance, "I have not yet begun to fight," uttered in a naval battle with the British during the American Revolutionary War. The episode made Jones an instant hero and earned him a place in history.

When the war of independence was over Congress disbanded the American navy, and the hero found himself unemployed. An incredibly egotistical man, Jones was disappointed that the new government did not reward him with an important position, so he drifted to Europe where he lived the life of a playboy, a role very much of his liking. He swept the ladies off their feet at the royal courts of kings and princes, winding up at Paris where he died in 1792, an old, worn-out man at 45. France at the time was busy with a major revolution of its own, and no record of Jones' funeral or burial service ever reached America. Thus ended, in oblivion, the story of a hero, John Paul Jones.

More than a century later in 1899, General Horace Porter was assigned as American ambassador to France, and he quickly made it his business to investigate the truth about John Paul Jones. After all, the American hero might have been murdered by one side or the other in the fierce Parisian riots of 1792. Porter's inquiry took six years to complete.

Embassy staff initiated a program of painstaking research into old French government archives and the surviving papers of private citizens, including the records of every doctor living in Paris in 1792. After three years, the first clue was uncovered — a tattered certificate saying that Jones' body was buried at St. Louis Cemetery, a graveyard once reserved for foreigners.

But no such cemetery could be located in all of Paris or the surrounding countryside. Further research revealed that such a place had once existed but had been long since abandoned. The original site was at last identified as a disreputable section of Paris, now covered over with mean streets and dilapidated slum housing.

Next came the task of battling French red tape, properly renowned as the reddest, most complex administrative fortress in the civilized world. Ambassador Porter eventually received permission to sink a series of shafts and tunnels in the yards and alleys of the dingy neighborhood. Prospects were uncertain. No plat or listing of names had been found for the old cemetery. Plenty of human bones were quickly uncovered at a depth of only three or four feet, not in the orderly arrangement of conventional gravesites, but tumbled helter-skelter together like so many jackstraws. Presumably these were the victims of street fighting in the bloody months of the revolution.

After three months of digging in this grisly underground mine, a plain lead casket with no exterior markings was brought to the surface. Ambassador Porter was summoned to the scene, and at a nearby medical college the heavy lid was raised in the presence of embassy personnel and French officials. Revealed to their astonished gaze was a male corpse in a remarkable state of preservation more than a century after burial.

Following death, the remains had been carefully wrapped in foil, immersed in a bath of alcohol, and packed securely with padding of hay and straw. The flesh was intact, but slightly shrunken and discolored.

Experts were summoned to take measurements and photographs for comparison with what was known of the physical characteristics of John Paul Jones in his lifetime. In delighted satisfaction, Ambassador Porter noted that everything seemed to match exactly.

Still another year passed in formalities and paperwork. Then in April 1906 the body was placed with appropriate pomp and ceremony in an impressive crypt under the chapel at the U.S. Naval Academy in Annapolis. Thus John Paul Jones was officially assigned to his final resting place. At least some people were pretty sure it was the body of John Paul Jones.

Long Funeral Leads to "Promised Land"

Of the many wagon trains making the long, slow journey over the western plains, the strangest of all was the procession led by William Keil. At Bethel, Missouri, on a May morning in 1855, the bearded, steely-eyed Keil took his place at the head of the line and sounded a blast on his trumpet, the signal to move out. The caravan consisted of 24 covered wagons loaded with families and their belongings and with assorted livestock tethered to the tailgates. Keil in the lead drove a four-mule team pulling a hearse containing the body of his eldest son Willie.

William Keil, an independent German preacher with a magnetic personality, founded a religious communal colony in Missouri in 1844. For about 10 years the community prospered with the members devoting their days to diligent work on the land and their evenings to religious music and prayer. However, as new settlers gradually drifted into Missouri from the Eastern seaboard, Keil felt that the world was closing in and that their beliefs and their unique way of life might be endangered. He promised his followers that he would establish a new colony far to the west in Washington Territory. He also promised his son Willie that, as heir, he could lead the pilgrimage to the new Promised Land in the West.

But as preparations went forward, Willie died suddenly, without warning. Refusing to break his promise, Keil made a massive casket of lead in which he placed the body, completely immersing it in alcohol.

Reports of Indian attacks on the plains were so alarming at the time that Keil's friends urged him not to start. Tales were told of thousands of Redskins robbing and destroying wagon trains all along the Oregon Trail, and according to rumor, the U.S. Army no longer had the power to provide protection. Keil refused to be intimidated, saying, "When I blow the trumpet, Willie moves ahead, and we follow him."

At every stop along the journey, the travelers were told of dangers ahead. The Redskin was once more master of the West. A band of 8,000 Indians had collected between Kearney and Laramie. An even larger force of 15,000 was encamped at the Big Blue River.

Undaunted by all warnings, Keil sounded the trumpet every morning at dawn and the mules pulling Willie's body stepped out to begin the day's march while the entire company raised their voices in hymns.

Indians were sighted frequently day after day, solitary mounted figures here and there on the hillsides, or as swift-moving patrols riding parallel with the wagon route. Always the watchers fled at the sound of Keil's trumpet blast. All too often the travelers encountered the wreckage of earlier trains, mute, grisly evidence of the ferocity of Indian attacks. Once a pair of daring Indians approached the train to beg for food, which was given, but throughout their visit the Redskins kept a fearful eye on the wagon at the head of the line.

The travelers were not exempt from the natural hazards of the trail. At times there was no water, and over miles of barren parched earth some of the livestock died. Finally, near the end of November, more than five months after leaving Missouri, the caravan reached Willapa, Washington. Here after a 2,000-mile funeral, Willie's body was at last laid to rest. The same mules drew the casket to the graveside, and a blast of the trumpet signaled the congregation to commence the final hymn.

Keil established a new communal colony in Oregon Territory, calling it Aurora after his daughter. Here too the settlers prospered as a result of hard work and devotion to their religious principles. In time the old man died, and once more the world moved in. A few years after the founder's decease, the communal settlement disappeared.

Were These Two Men One and the Same?

This is the story of two men. One was a great soldier whose exploits brighten the pages of European military history. The other was a quiet schoolmaster, a gentle man who tutored the children of South Carolina families, who died about 20 years before the Civil War.

Historians on both sides of the ocean, in France and England as well as America, still debate the question: Were these two men, so different in so many ways, actually and in fact the same person?

In the early part of the last century, the Emperor Napoleon set out to conquer all of Europe, and almost succeeded. The greatest and most talented commander in Napoleon's army was Marshal Michel Ney.

It was Ney who led the armies of Napoleon to their greatest victories, and it was Ney who saved French forces from annihilation when defeat put an end to Napoleonic dreams of conquest. During the final battle against the British at Waterloo in June 1815, Ney had three horses shot out from under him.

Though his clothes were riddled by bullets, he remained unwounded and fought on foot until nightfall in the midst of the slain.

When it was all over and Napoleon was consigned to exile for life, Marshal Ney was captured by forces of the King of France and tried by court martial for treason because of his role in the Napoleonic uprising. The sentence was death, and according to official French army records General Ney was executed by a firing squad on Dec. 7, 1815, in the gardens of the Luxembourg palace. So ended the career of a great soldier. On Jan. 16, 1816, a ship docked in Charleston, S.C., having sailed from the French port of Bordeaux nearly a month earlier on Christmas Day. Three passengers disembarked. One of them was a tall man with square shoulders and the military carriage of a soldier trained in the saddle.

For three days after the landing, rumors circulating among the French population of Charleston whispered that the tall stranger was a Frenchman of importance who had escaped from the postwar turmoil then engulfing Paris.

When a French veteran of the Napoleonic wars, slightly intoxicated, encountered the stranger in a tavern, he addressed the tall man as "General" and saluted him as his former commander. Curtly the big man turned his back, saying that a mistake had been made. From then on, the stranger was no longer seen on the streets of the city.

In the old South, long before public schools were established, it was customary for prominent plantation families to hire private teachers who lived in the household and conducted classes for children in the vicinity.

Sometimes in the early 1820s, a tall scholarly man with a soft voice and scars on his face occupied such a position in the home of Col. Benjamin Rogers near Cheraw in Marlboro County. An excellent teacher, the man spoke French and English with equal fluency. He was familiar with the classics and was an authority on European history. He said his name was Peter Stuart Ney.

When people became too friendly or inquired too closely into his past, he simply packed his few belongings to seek employment at a new location.

In 1843 the quiet teacher was back in South Carolina at the plantation home of Robert Rogers, just a few miles from the present day city of Florence. The schoolhouse where he taught, restored by the present landowner, still stands on the estate of Evander M. Ervin — a monument to the memory of the mysterious stranger.

He died in 1846, and scholars since then have been puzzling over the secret. A dozen books have been written on the subject.

Then in 1885, a very old lady who had attended school under Ney as a small girl wrote that in her youth she had formed a warm friendship with the uncommunicative stranger. He confided in her, giving details in his early life, admitting that Peter Ney the schoolteacher was in fact the former Marshal Michel Ney of France.

According to her account, the French firing squad of 1815 refused to kill their former commander, and after firing over his head helped him to escape by sea.

Is this tale the romantic fantasy of a sentimental old woman whose memory cannot be trusted? Nobody knows for sure. There the matter rests. The question is still unanswered.

They Played a Dangerous Game — and Lost

One of the best fighting groups of the American war with Mexico was the Company of Saint Patrick, an artillery unit renowned for its valor in standing fast under heavy enemy fire. Most of the members were Irishmen, immigrants who had left the poverty of Ireland behind in search of a better life in the New World. They were also deserters from the U.S. Army and they fought on the side of Mexico.

The story begins in the winter of 1845-46 when Brigadier General Zachary Taylor moved his army into the newly annexed land of Texas in preparation for war with Mexico. In the encampment near the mouth of the Rio Grande, troops were subjected to several months of miserable existence under virtually intolerable conditions. Weather was cold and wet; tenting and boots were both shoddy. Food was bad and drinking water was salty. Stupid and inexperienced officers attempted to maintain discipline by imposing degrading forms of physical punishment for the slightest infractions of military regulations by enlisted soldiers. Dysentery and other diseases flourished, and as morale sagged, desertions became frequent. Mexican military authorities, seeking to capitalize on these deficiencies, spread the word that any American soldier wishing to change sides would be rewarded with Mexican citizenship and 320 acres of free land after hostilities had ended.

Among the earliest of these Irishmen to swim the Rio Grande to Mexico was John Riley, a U.S. drill sergeant with a promising future. He was destined to distinguish himself further as a skillful leader directing the Company of Saint Patrick in battle. This strange foreign legion of Irish ex-patriates first saw action as an organized unit in the Battle of Buena Vista in February 1847. With textbook precision worthy of West Point, the Saint Pats set up their guns under the great green banner bearing the image of Ireland's patron saint, a harp emblematic of traditional Irish culture, and the shamrock, a universal badge of Irish ethnic solidarity. Casualties for the Saint Patricks were heavy in that first major engagement, but after the battle the unit was commended by General Santa Anna himself and Riley was promoted from lieutenant to captain.

As U.S. forces under Major General Winfield Scott penetrated deep into Mexico, the Saint Pats were moved into line under Santa Anna to help check the American drive on Mexico City. They fought their last action at the Battle of Churubusco as part of a small Mexican defense force facing a mammoth invading army. Repeatedly the guns of the Saint Pats drove the attackers back, but the weight of numbers proved to be critical. While other Mexican units in turn raised white flags of surrender, the Irishmen continued to fight. When their ammunition was exhausted they met the Americans with bayonets. Of the company of more than 200, only 85 survived, and these — including John Riley — were taken as prisoners.

All were tried by court martial as deserters, and most were sentenced to death. General Scott personally reviewed each case and reduced the sentences of a few. Sixty were eventually hanged, but Riley escaped death on the technicality that he had deserted from the U.S. Army prior to the formal declaration of war against Mexico in May 1846. His sentence was reduced to 50 lashes with a rawhide whip and branding. The branding consisted of a capital "D" two inches high burned into the cheekbone with a red-hot iron.

When the treaty ending the war with Mexico was enacted in February 1848, Santa Anna bargained for the release of the surviving members of the Company of Saint Patrick. Riley returned to the Mexican army and later rose to the rank of colonel. Sometime later a monument to the valor of the Saint Pats was erected by the side of a road near Mexico City. It was fashioned in the form of a cross inscribed with three symbols: a gamecock, depicting outstanding fighting qualities and tenacity; a pair of dice, representing the gamble they took; and the universal totem of death, the skull and crossbones.

Pony Express Provided Thrills — for a While

A brief but exciting morsel of American frontier history survives in the saga of the Pony Express. The story began in 1860 when the great freighting company of Russell, Majors, and Wadell undertook to provide fast mail service from St. Joseph, Missouri, to San Francisco, California. St. Jo at the time was the outermost station of eastern civilization. During the next 19 months the riders of the Pony Express galloped 650,000 miles on the eight-to-ten day schedule from east to west. They traveled through territory as yet untamed, where hostile Indians and wild animals were but two of the hazards to be met and overcome. Even the wagon trains moving slowly west were not always friendly to the riders since it was believed they sometimes attracted unwelcome attention from the savages.

Some of the riders were former mule skinners, tough stage drivers, and rough cowboys, but the majority was composed of restless farm boys, most of them still in their teens. On joining the service, each new rider was obliged to take an oath swearing to refrain from using profane language or the use of intoxicating liquor. Each man also was given a small leather-bound Bible which he carried in his bedroll. The pay was adequate for 1860, $50 a month plus board, but the company spent more for the horses — nothing but the very best would do — and for this reason the riders were nearly always able to out-distance their Indian pursuers. Since the postage charged by the company for the 2,000-mile trip was $5 per half ounce, Pony Express carried only mail of significant importance, including government communications from Washington.

Among the many tales of the Pony Express handed down over the years there is the story of Billy Tate, 14, who sold his life dearly when he was ambushed by a blood-thirsty band of mounted Indians. In a running firefight young Billy brought down seven of the Redskins before he himself was fatally shot and toppled from the saddle. The pony with the mail pouches securely in place got through alone to the next relay station. Another rider, his name now forgotten, leaped from the saddle to safety as his pony stumbled over the edge of a cliff in Utah. It took him 20 minutes to climb down into the ravine to retrieve the mail and two hours to climb out. He then walked the remaining eight miles to the relay station where he collapsed in exhaustion. It was William Fisher, a young Mormon rider with the Pony Express, who first uttered the classic slogan, "The Mail Must Go Through." When a howling blizzard isolated the relay station, and travel seemed impossible, William insisted on moving forward even when he had to lead the pony by the bridle through the swirling storm. He made it to his assigned destination, a few hours late, but lost fingers and toes due to frostbite.

Perhaps even more vulnerable to the dangers of the Wild West were the men who ran the relay station where fresh horses and food were available for the riders. These crews of two or three men attempted to maintain friendly relations with neighboring Indians, but the Redmen were frequently unpredictable. During bad weather when food was scarce, or when a warrior needed a new horse, trouble could be expected. Clashes were frequent, and a score or more of stations were burned to ashes. Remarkably, however, fatalities at the stations were few.

The Pony Express was put out of business by completion of the transcontinental telegraph in 1862. According to company claims, the operation lost $200,000 during the year and a half of its existence. The early promise of a government subsidy from Washington never materialized.

As for the surviving riders, most of them faded away into the obscurity of ordinary respectable lives. Many saw service with the cavalry on one side or the other. Of the glamorous brotherhood, only one — Buffalo Bill Cody — went on to capitalize on the spirit of adventure and daring that was the very essence of the Old West.

A Little Salt Caused a Lot of Trouble in Texas

The war between the United States and Mexico ended in 1848, but full-scale hostilities almost erupted again in 1877. At issue was the price of salt in Texas, and Mexicans and Americans died before the matter was settled.

About a hundred miles west of El Paso, in the triangle formed by the Rio Grande and the border of New Mexico, lies a bleak desert valley composed of white alkali flats and saline lakes. For years after the war of the 1840s was over, Mexican peasants from both sides of the Rio Grande continued to drive their creaky oxcarts into the desert, bringing them back loaded with salt. The salt was a natural resource available to all, and numbers of villages along the river depended on it for their livelihood.

Then in 1877, Judge Charles H. Howard of El Paso staked out a claim on the salt flats, claiming exclusive rights to the saline deposits. Under Texas law his claim was legal, but the action created an immediate uproar. Mexican protests were at first more noisy than violent, but a crisis was soon reached when in September 1877 the judge ordered the arrest of several Mexicans for stealing salt. Immediately a mob converged on the jail at San Elizario, the county seat of El Paso, and not only freed the culprits but made prisoners of Judge Howard and the sheriff. At a summary trial in the town square the mob found the Texas judge responsible for all the grievances suffered by Mexicans since the conquest of their land by the gringos. Without a doubt Howard would have been hanged there and then were it not for the appearance of Luis Cardis, a prominent and highly respected leader of the Mexican community in Texas. After extensive pleading, Cardis talked the mob into a compromise. Howard's life would be spared if he would relinquish his claim to the salt flats and leave Texas forever. With no choice in the matter, Howard agreed and left for New Mexico.

Perversely, however, Howard blamed his humiliation on Cardis, the man who had saved his life. A month later the angry judge was back in El Paso with a double-barreled shotgun looking for the

Mexican leader. When they met in a general store, Howard fired both barrels at point-blank range.

Wasting no further time in El Paso, Howard then rode hard to the capital at Austin where he demanded that Governor Hubbard give him military protection for his legitimate business interests. The governor had no military help to offer. Fort Bliss at El Paso had been closed years earlier. Instead Hubbard authorized recruitment of a small band of Rangers to satisfy Howard's request.

Thus it was that in December 1877 Judge Howard once more approached El Paso accompanied by two business partners and his small army of two dozen Rangers. At the town of San Elizario they were met by a force of several hundred armed and angry Mexicans. Outnumbered and outgunned, the Rangers and their chargers took refuge in a small adobe building to fight for their lives. For five days, with unhurried precision, the Mexicans kept the small improvised fort under fire. Finally, with food and ammunition gone, the Rangers were forced to raise the white flag of surrender. Under the flag of truce the Rangers were disarmed. Their horses were restored to them; a few parting shots in the air from the Mexican rabble hastened their ignominious departure from the town of San Elizario. Judge Howard and his partners were stood against a wall and summarily shot.

Alarmed by the frightening news from west Texas, officials in Washington were spooked into action. The nation was in no way prepared for another war with Mexico. Fort Bliss at El Paso was hurriedly reactivated, and a garrison of federal troops was sent to establish the government presence and maintain the peace. No member of the avenging Mexican vigilante army was ever apprehended. Forever after, however, as each creaking oxcart made its way into the desert for a load of salt, the peasant operator was required to pay a fee for the privilege to the sovereign state of Texas.

Heroic Flyer Earned Small Place in History

John Silver served with the U.S. Army for almost 18 years. During all that time he held no rank and received no pay. Yet when he finally died at a ripe old age, he was permanently and honorably memorialized by military authorities.

The story of John Silver dates back to 1918 in France when American doughboys were locked in combat with the Kaiser's German army. At that time radio had not come into widespread use for field communications, and telephone wires strung along ditches and hedges were frequently chewed up by tanks and trucks. John Silver was a pigeon employed in the task of carrying messages from the front lines to headquarters camps in the rear.

According to official U.S. Army records, John Silver was hatched in January 1918 at a pigeon loft behind American lines in France. In his first few weeks as he learned to fly he became accustomed to a small metal canister strapped to one leg, the container which later would carry important military messages. When training was completed, John Silver was assigned to a front-line infantry unit for courier duty.

On October 21, 1918, the famous Meuse-Argonne offensive had just begun, and it was essential that command headquarters — 25 miles to the rear — be notified of the rapidly changing battlefield situation. The Germans were laying down an unexpectedly intense artillery barrage.

With the canister of vital information strapped to his leg, John Silver was released from his coop. Tense soldiers watched anxiously as the bird first fluttered uncertainly. The lives of the men could depend on the pigeon. When John Silver leveled-off at treetop height and turned in the right direction, the men cheered.

Suddenly the cheer was displaced by a groan of dismay as observers saw a German shell explode very close to the tiny figure.

Half an hour later, John Silver flopped into his home loft at battalion headquarters with his message intact. A machinegun bullet had ripped his chest, and bits of shrapnel had torn the tender flesh.

His right leg was missing but the precious canister was still dangling from the broken left leg.

When the war was over, the Army shipped John Silver to Hawaii where he joined 240 other pigeons in a training school at Schofield Barracks.

Some years later when General Henry H. "Hap" Arnold established the Air Force museum at Wright-Patterson Field, John Silver became one of the first items placed on display. He still stands erect on a roost in the Hall of Fame at the world's largest aviation museum above a small plaque telling his story of his heroism.

Wild West Bandit Defied Lawmen for Years

One of the last stage robbers of the Old West eluded the best efforts of Wells Fargo detectives for years before he was finally trapped by accident. Through all his long career of successful robberies, the bandit always used the same plan of operation and was never known to use a horse.

It all began in Calaveras County, California, on a July day in 1875. The stage from Sonora to Milton was slowly climbing a steep mountain road as driver Bill Hodges cracked his whip over the heads of his six sweating horses. Near the crest of the hill, a tall man stepped out of the trees into the road. He was dressed in a long linen duster reaching to his boots. A loose hood with two eye holes covered his face and in his hands he brandished a double-barreled shotgun.

"Throw down the box, sir," he ordered quietly, and Bill Hodges remembered later that the voice was modulated, even courteous. Producing a hatchet from under his cloak, the robber smashed open the chest and stuffed the $300 contents in his pocket. Waving the shotgun then, he ordered the driver to whip up his horses.

When a posse from Milton reached the scene, they found the shattered box and some lines of verse scribbled on the back of the Wells Fargo bill of lading.

> *I've labored long and hard for bread,*
> *For honor and for riches,*
> *But on my toes too long you've tread,*
> *You fine-haired sons of bitches*
> *(If this line is considered offensive*
> *it may be changed to read: Now your*
> *money's in my britches.)*
> *Signed Black Bart PO8*

Five months later, Black Bart struck again, intercepting the stage from San Juan to Marysville, and a few weeks later the robber in the white hood turned up miles away at Roseburg. The technique was the same in each case. As the horses slowed to a walk near the top of a steep hill, the bandit stepped out with shotgun pointed at the driver's chest. No clues were ever found except the lines of verse — different each time — and the signature: Black Bart PO8. Newspapers made a big splash of the bandit who composed poetry, printing every line for the edification of readers.

After half a dozen robberies, the chief of Wells Fargo police took personal charge of the case, but his investigation turned up nothing. For the next eight years the faceless, horseless bandit plagued the Wells Fargo stage routes all over California. In November 1883 Black Bart returned to the scene of his first crime on the road to Sonora. According to rumor, the treasure box on the stage was particularly well filled on this trip.

The driver that day was accompanied by a youngster named Jimmy who came along to try out his new rifle on rabbits or prairie dogs by the roadside. When the horses slowed near the top of the hill and Black Bart stepped out of the trees, young Jimmy recklessly fired a wild shot. To the surprise of both men, the bandit turned tail and fled into the woods. But in his haste to escape, the hooded figure dropped a handkerchief bearing the laundry mark FX07 — at long last a clue to the identity of Black Bart.

Wells Fargo detectives traced the handkerchief to a laundry in San Francisco where it was identified as the property of Mr. C. E. Bolton, a respected citizen of the city. After his arrest the officers asked the meaning of the mysterious symbol PO8 which appeared at the end of his poetic compositions. "That PO8," explained Black Bart, "stands for poet."

Although Black Bart committed 28 stage robberies in all, he was tried for only the last one, the unlucky event at which he dropped his handkerchief. He was released from San Quentin prison in January 1888 and was never seen or heard from after that time.

Luck Ran Out for this Soldier of Fortune

For red-blooded Americans with a taste for adventure, the middle of the 19th century was a great time to be alive. Following the annexation of Texas and a victorious war against Mexico in the 1840s, the whole Southwest came under the U.S. Flag. Oregon was opened up for settlement about the same time, and gold was discovered in California in 1849. America was expanding rapidly and numbers of adventuresome young men were eager to promote the national destiny without benefit of approval from the government in Washington.

Such a man was William Walker of Nashville, a doctor-lawyer-newsman who believed that America had a duty to acquire and pacify the war-torn republics of Central America. In stature he was really a little fellow, a short-freckled-face youth with yellow hair. His eyes were his distinctive feature, steely gray and penetrating. In his short career as a soldier of fortune, Walker became known as the gray-eyed man of destiny.

Walker's first venture at empire building took place in 1853 when with 40 followers he descended on Lower California and declared that part of Mexico an independent republic. When popular support among Mexicans failed to materialize, the expedition ran out of supplies and the band retreated back to the United States. A San Francisco jury declined to convict Walker of violating U.S. neutrality laws.

Next in 1855 with a force of 50 freebooters, Walker invaded Nicaragua, then in the throes of a civil war. The invaders attached themselves to the underdog side and after fierce fighting succeeded in taking possession of the capital city of Granada. Walker declared himself president and appointed his men to high government positions as he set out to bring social reform to the tiny country. But his dictatorial policies soon created a host of new enemies. Early in 1856 the neighboring republic of Costa Rica declared war on the Walker bandit government. Other neighboring states — Guatemala, El Salvador, and Honduras — joined in the invasion.

For several months the fighting was bitter and bloody, but Walker and his men were finally trapped as resistance became hopeless. In their final hours they systematically destroyed the city of Granada. Walker himself escaped to the coast where he boarded an American warship. A hero's welcome awaited him when he arrived in New Orleans.

In spite of all this misfortune, Walker's dream was not dead nor was his courage exhausted. The final invasion of his career was launched in June 1860 when he landed with 80 men on the coast of Honduras. In vain he attempted to incite the people to join him in overthrowing the government, but for months he managed to inflict serious casualties on defending forces. Early in September Walker was encamped near the coast on the bank of the Rio Negro when he found himself trapped between the sea and a force of 900 Honduran troops. Once more Walker tried to extricate himself by seeking refuge on a warship — this time a British sloop anchored at the mouth of the river. With Walker on board the vessel steamed up to the city of Truxillo where the Britishers turned the soldier of fortune over to Honduran authorities.

During his short stay in prison Walker had little to say and on September 12 walked quietly to the place of his execution in the city plaza. A chair was placed against the wall, and Walker declining a bandage for his eyes sat down to face a firing squad of 10 riflemen. He spoke just a few words before the end, exonerating his followers of all blame and assuming full responsibility for all that had happened. His voice bore no hint of remorse or self-pity as luck ran out for the gray-eyed man of destiny before he reached age 36.

Ship Disaster on Mississippi Was Avoidable

The worst shipwreck in American history did not take place on a stormy ocean but on the relatively placid waters of the Mississippi River. Because the tragedy was overshadowed by two other monumental events in the same month, the nation's press gave little space to the staggering loss of life. The vessel involved was the paddle-steamer *Sultana* which blew up and burned at 1 a.m. on April 27, 1865, just upriver from Memphis.

By the middle of April 1865 the War Between the States was over and President Lincoln was dead. Military men on both sides were engaged in the business of recovering prisoners of war and bringing them home to whatever destiny was left for them. As part of this process Confederate forces at Vicksburg, Mississippi, released about 2,000 prisoners to the custody of the Union Army. When the bright new side-wheeler *Sultana* pulled into Vicksburg on her regular run upriver from New Orleans to St. Louis, Union officers requisitioned the vessel to transport the prisoners north. Apparently nobody bothered to check the total capacity of the craft or the extent of sanitary facilities available. As the troops were herded up the gangplank like so many cattle, it became clear to observers that the ship would be overloaded. In addition to the human burden of 1,900 men was added the load of 60 horses and 100 hogs. The weight was so great that the upper deck sagged in spite of the many stanchions erected to support it. The men on board could barely move about during the day and not at all at night. Cooking arrangements were wholly inadequate. One small wood stove on the upper deck was supposed to suffice. Some of the more enterprising troops soon learned how to draw hot water from the ship's boiler to warm their rations.

In spite of these hardships, the men were generally in a cheerful mood at the prospect of going home with the war behind. If any of them felt they were being treated harshly by their own people, no complaints were reported.

Although the *Sultana* was in tiptop mechanical condition,

progress was slow in her overburdened state. Everyone except crew members was asleep when catastrophe struck. Through the inky darkness the ship was paddling hard against the current when without hint of warning the boiler exploded with thunderous roar. Bodies were tossed high in the air and screams resounded when fire swept with the speed of light through the length and breadth of the decks. Scores of men simply leaped overboard to perish in the icy water. Others fought for possession of a plank, a chair, anything that would float. Those who could swim struck out for shore in the light of the inferno of fire. Of the 1,900 persons on board the *Sultana* on her final voyage, 1,238 lost their lives as a result of explosion, fire or drowning.

Major General N. T. Dana was appointed to head the military investigation, but the board of officers assigned no blame and ordered no punishment. In spite of pleas by some of the survivors to the Congress, this verdict was permitted to stand. One critical question was never fully explored. As the *Sultana* was taking on her tremendous burden of human cargo at Vicksburg on April 24, 1865, another paddle-wheel steamer of similar size was tied up at a nearby dock, empty and available for use. A routine requisition by military authority could have placed the *Pauline Carroll* at the service of the prisoners on their journey home. Why did officers of the Union Army elect to use only the ill-fated *Sultana* for transport of the troops?

Big Gun at Naval Academy Memorializes Classic Error

On the grounds of the U.S. Naval Academy at Annapolis stands an old naval cannon known as the Oregon. The big gun was once one of a pair, the companion piece bearing the name Peacemaker. However, the Peacemaker is not on display because it blew up in 1844 and almost wiped out the executive branch of the U.S. government.

These two powerful guns were the principal armament of the *U.S.S. Princeton* when she was launched at Philadelphia in 1843. Commanded by Captain Robert F. Stockton, USN, the *Princeton* was at once the most modern steamship in the world and the most heavily armed frigate of any navy. She was the first large vessel to be driven by a screw propeller instead of paddlewheels and was the first to burn smokeless anthracite coal. She had a telescoping smokestack that could be lowered to prevent interference with the sails when she was not using her engines. Captain Stockton was justifiably proud of his new command. He had supervised construction at every step of the way, and being a wealthy man, had contributed to the cost of the ship from his own pocket.

As for the big guns, each could toss a 225-pound ball for several miles, but they were not a matched pair. Oregon was designed and forged in England, while Stockton himself had designed Peacemaker, forged of finest American wrought iron. Peacemaker was also the larger of the two with a gross weight of 133 tons. Understandably, the commander considered his own gun to be superior.

Following a shakedown cruise, Captain Stockton proudly sailed the *Princeton* up the Potomac to Washington in February 1844. Several days were then spent in showing off the ultramodern ship and its equipment to the President, cabinet members, congressmen, senators, and other dignitaries. Always the mighty Peacemaker was used for firepower demonstrations, while Oregon remained silent and unheeded.

A week later Stockton issued an invitation to about 400 of the very best people in the nation's capital to spend a day aboard the *Princeton*. Guests included President John Tyler and several members of his family, all cabinet officers except the Secretary of the Treasury, numerous high-ranking navy officers, many members of Congress, as well as ministers and ambassadors from the diplomatic corps. Ladies included the famous Dolley Madison and Miss Julia Gardiner who later became the President's second wife, as well as wives, daughters and fiancees of the distinguished gentlemen. On the sunny cruise down the river, Peacemaker was fired several times, and the company was properly impressed.

Near Mount Vernon the ship dropped anchor and everyone was ushered below decks for a gala luncheon. Of course the food was superb and champagne flowed freely. The President toasted the Navy, Captain Stockton, and the Peacemaker, while the commander responded in kind. In mid-afternoon some of the guests requested a final demonstration of the big gun, and Stockton after some persuasion finally agreed. With festivities at their height, however, only a dozen men, and no women at all, decided to go up on deck to witness the firing. President Tyler with one hand on the rail and a foot on the bottom stair waited to hear the end of a song being sung by his son-in-law.

With the gun crew in position and the guests ranged along the rail, Stockton shouted the order: "Fire!" A thunderous roar followed and the ship trembled from stem to stern as a cloud of dense smoke enveloped the scene. As the smoke lifted a fearsome vista of carnage was revealed. The great gun had burst asunder about three feet forward of the breech. A 20-foot gap in the rail marked the path of a piece of metal weighing nearly a ton. Another piece of similar size shattered into fragments and sprayed the port side of the deck like a barrage of shrapnel. Secretary of State Abel P. Upshur and Secretary of the Navy Thomas W. Gilmer died instantly. Ambassador Virgil Maxcey, New York Senator David Gardiner, and Captain Beverly Kennon, Chief of Naval Construction, were dead within minutes, as were two members of the gun crew and the President's personal valet. The other spectators were thrown to the deck by the force of the explosion.

A Navy board of inquiry absolved Captain Stockton of all blame for the accident, finding that the explosion was caused by a fault in the metal of the gun. The Oregon saw service with the Navy for another 20 years before being placed in retirement at the Naval Academy. Today the big gun stands, silent and unheeded as before, as a mute memorial to the vanity of men and the penalty that must inevitably be paid for excessive pride.

Camel Corps Put Strange Beast in Southwest

As the U.S. Army pushed westward with the frontier in the early 1800s, transport proved to be a major problem. In the old Spanish Southwest particularly, wagon wheels sank into the desert sand, water was forever scarce, and the searing heat tested the endurance of men and mules.

As early as 1836 someone suggested that the Army use camels, traditional beasts of burden of Arabia with legendary qualities of strength and durability under adverse conditions. Senator Jefferson Davis of Mississippi drafted legislation on the subject in 1851. Then when Davis became Secretary of War under President Millard Fillmore in 1853 he vigorously promoted the project and persuaded Congress to appropriate $30,000 for acquisition of a pilot group.

A military procurement team was sent to Egypt in 1855, and the first shipment of U.S. Army camels was landed at Indianola, Texas, in the spring of 1856. The herd included both dromedaries (one hump) and Bactrian camels (two humps), but the army simplified things by classifying them all as camels. Prices for the beasts ranged from $100 to $400, with the the top dollar going for a fine Arabian heavy with calf.

First reports from the training camp near San Antonio were highly encouraging. With an air of complete unconcern each camel could carry a packload of 300 pounds in torrential rain or desert heat, while covering 60 miles in two days. Unfortunately the beasts had a bad smell; they could be stubborn at times, and the other animals in camp avoided them. However, a second shipment from Egypt was delivered to bring the strength of the camel corps up to 70 animals.

The best test came in 1857 when Lieutenant Edward Beale was assigned to survey the route for a new wagon trail from Fort Defiance, New Mexico, to the coast of California. As Beale's expedition traveled through desert, mountain and wilderness, the camels hauled water for mules and men, partaking of very little for themselves. While the mules fed upon corn and oats, the camels ate off the land; prickly pear, greasewood, thorny bushes, and were completely content with their fare. At the end of 48 days, Beale, perched on the hump of a white camel, led a troop of mounted cameleers triumphantly into the streets of Los Angeles.

Beale's successful mission and vindication of the camel in military transport won him a permanent assignment. For the next four years the lieutenant and his camel corps wandered all over the Southwest on surveying assignments for the War Department.

Outbreak of the War Between the States was the beginning of the end for the camels. The army had no money for experimental projects. For a time the beasts were used to move freight from place to place in California, but some post commanders refused to allow the smelly, cantankerous animals into camp. A number of them escaped into the desert to live in the wild.

When the war was over, 44 camels remained of the original 70, and these were sold for $31 each. A few went to zoos and a few went to farmers who hoped, in vain, to break them to the plow. These too soon found their freedom in the deserts of California.

For many years after, old desert miners claimed that they frequently saw camels roaming in the wilderness, sometimes silhouetted against the setting sun, the last survivors of the American camel corps founded by Jefferson Davis.

U.S. Subsidized Karl Marx

The current generation of Americans has recently become more acutely aware of the global conflict with communism and its uncountable cost in treasure and human life. Because of events in the Caribbean and the Middle East, a new curiosity has arisen about the philosophical nature of Marxism with its deep-seated antipathy towards democracy and the West.

As every schoolboy knows, Karl Marx was the 19th century German thinker who formulated the doctrine of communism and devoted his life to preaching revolution. Less well known is the fact that Marx was subsidized in his writing for more than a decade by a New York newspaper. Without this support the world might never have seen the Marx blueprint for a new social order in which the rights of the individual are so rigorously denied.

In 1848 when Europe was living through a period of social unrest, Marx published his famous Communist Manifesto: "Workers of the World, Arise! You Have Nothing to Lose but Your Chains!" The workers of Europe did not respond to this call for revolution, but the document caught the attention of Horace Greeley, editor of New York's most distinguished newspaper, the *Tribune.* When Marx was banished as an undesirable from Europe and settled with his family in a shabby apartment in London, Greeley hired the revolutionist as special correspondent to the *Tribune.*

On Saturday, October 25, 1851, the paper published a special four-page supplement introducing this new, gifted philosopher to the American public. Greeley himself wrote a glowing editorial for the occasion, ignoring such domestic issues as a great Temperance Movement rally and a campaign promoting Daniel Webster for President of the United States.

The arrangement between Marx and the *Tribune* lasted for a full ten years, and the correspondent was apparently given free rein. Marx introduced some new words to America, words like "bourgeoisie" and "proletariat" as he interpreted the news of the day from the revolutionary viewpoint. In addition to being a philosopher, the German was a master of rhetoric. His attacks on capitalism and the upper classes were devastating in their eloquence.

While the *Tribune* was known as a respectable family paper, voice of the rising Republican party, the radical ideas of Marx were not altogether out of place in its pages. Greeley had a tendency to attract unconventional writers for the edification of New Yorkers. Articles sometimes supported vegetarianism, utopian communes, graham flour, and trousers for women.

The paper paid Marx $5 for each weekly article, a niggardly sum even for those days. Marx himself called it a "lousy capitalist pittance" and kept begging for an increase. During those years, this lousy capitalist pittance was the only source of income for the philosopher as he struggled to keep his family alive on bread and potatoes. No one in England or on the Continent would offer employment to this outcast who was under the continuing surveillance by the police of several countries. Nevertheless Marx submitted his articles faithfully, each one ending with the inevitable refrain on the approach of the sweeping revolution that would erase the evils of capitalism and transform the world into a workers' Garden of Eden.

Throughout those years of privation in the squalor of a London slum, Marx toiled over his major life's work, the massive volume, *Das Kapital*, that was to become the bible of the world communist movement. Numbers of lively minds in the United States had already begun to examine this new gospel of socialism, even finding a religious flavor in its ideals. But the more responsible among them were dubious about the complete and violent overthrow of the existing social structure. However as the monumental task of putting his ideas on paper neared completion, so too did Marx's association with the *Tribune* approach termination.

In the United States during the 1850s, interest in world affairs began to wane as attention was focused on the series of crises leading up to the Civil War. Marx and his dream of a communist paradise faded into the background as the spectre of armed contlict haunted America.

A polite letter from Greeley to Marx explained the need for a reduction in the number of foreign correspondents. In another letter Marx called Greeley a "lousy bum," but the relationship was over. However, the work on *Das Kapital* was finished, and the communist genie was out of the bottle. Marx died in 1886 smugly confident that his blueprint for world reform would soon bring revolution to the industrialized countries of Europe. Never did he dream that Marxism would first find expression in Russia, a backward, barbarian country he thoroughly despised.

Daydreams about the "might-have-been" can do nothing to alter the past, but it is nonetheless interesting to speculate on what direction history might have taken without the influence of *Das Kapital* and the role of Horace Greeley in making completion of the work possible.

Dickens' Visit to U.S. Stirs Emotional Reactions

When Charles Dickens visited the United States in 1842, some Americans exerted a strenuous effort to give the popular English novelist the spectacular kind of reception they considered appropriate to the occasion. Dickens with his wife Kate debarked from their ship at Boston, and the city in celebration renamed itself Boz-town, borrowing the pen name "Boz" used by the author in his earlier works. Highlight of the sequence of social events over the next several days was a gala stag dinner at which spirits were served copiously. (In those days spirits were never served in the presence of ladies.)

A committee of New Yorkers preparing to receive the distinguished visitor decided to out-do Boz-town by staging the greatest party in the history of their party-loving city. Advertised as the Boz Ball, the colossal event was scheduled for Valentine's Day at the Park Theater, largest gathering place in New York with an estimated capacity of about 3,000 people. Tickets were sold at $5 per person, and for a surcharge of $2 a gentleman could bring an extra lady. Days in advance, every ticket was sold, with wealthy New Yorkers offering as much as $40 for the precious pasteboards without success.

No expense was spared on the preparations and decorations. The interior of the theater was modified to provide maximum space for dancing. Elaborate chandeliers hung by golden ropes were suspended from the ceiling. Flowers, draperies, and 7,000 yards of bunting — together with the flags of all states — adorned the walls. For three days and nights in advance of the great day, 150 men and women worked to prepare refreshments.

Brilliantly conceived and expertly managed, the affair left nothing to be desired. Dickens himself commented on how well the police handled the congested carriage traffic converging on the theater. A lady guest later wrote a friend that the crowd consumed, among other things, 50 smoked hams, 50 beef tongues, 40,000 oysters raw and pickled, and 10,000 chocolate bonbons. A corps of 70 waiters circulated among the guests bearing trays of champagne, tea and hot chocolate. Following his formal welcome by the mayor of New York, Dickens and his young wife kept pace with the festivities almost to the very end.

When at last it was over, the committee of promoters surveyed the scene with satisfaction. Bunting, flags and special lights were all in place; very few of the 4,000 plates and 5,000 glasses had been broken. In a stroke of perverted genius the promoters decided to repeat the Boz Ball for a second night — and at half price for the benefit of disappointed New Yorkers who had been unable to obtain tickets for the first presentation. Once the decision was announced, the new issue of tickets was snapped up by enthusiastic buyers. The mayor and other political personages agreed to return for the repeat performance. Stores of refreshments were replenished. But even as the crowds once more converged in their carriages on the Park Theater, a devastaging message arrived from Dickens at his hotel. The distinguished British visitor was confined to his bed with a bad cold and a sore throat. His appearance at the second Boz Ball was out of the question.

In panic now, and fearing a riot by angry New Yorkers, the committee sent an urgent message to Dickens asking for a doctor's certificate testifying that he was indeed incapacitated by illness. No further mention of any such certificate can be found.

Nevertheless, the party went on with typical New York exuberance and dancing till the first streaks of dawn appeared over the city. It is even possible that nobody missed the honored guest. But for the rest of his American tour, Charles Dickens, the beloved Boz, made a point of declining all public receptions in his honor. This decision, unfortunately, caused some resentment in American communities he later visited. But that's the way it is, and human nature hasn't changed all that much in 140 years or so.

Newsmen Demonstrate Power of the Press

Many tales can be told of promotional activities devised by newspaper editors to arouse or stimulate community interest. One of the best of these concerns Benjamin Day of the old New York *Sun* who with his star reporter Richard Locke provided dramatic coverage on new scientific studies of the moon. Day was eager for a boost in circulation, while Locke hoped for an increase in his $12-a-week salary.

As it so happened in 1835, the world-famous astronomer Sir John Herschel was conducting stellar observations from the Cape of Good Hope at the tip of South Africa. However, ship sailings between New York and South Africa were few and far between in those days, and of course there was no telegraph or cable service at the time. These details did not deter Day and Locke from providing their readers with comprehensive coverage of some amazing new advances in science.

Locke's first story on a Friday in August gave a factual account of Herschel's scholarly background and went on to describe in detail the construction of a great new (wholly imaginary) astronomical telescope. After giving full technical details, the story concluded with a "quote" from Herschel saying that the new telescope was powerful enough to detect the presence of insect life on the moon. The impact of this report on readers of a penny newspaper in 1835 can only be imagined.

After a decent interval of a few days, the paper came out with descriptions of some things observed with the new telescope. Under the headline "Animal Life on Moon," reporter Locke moved to fresh heights of creativity. With a generous sprinkling of scientific jargon, he told of sparkling white beaches, mountains of green marble, and trees with feather-like foliage. Among these hills and trees were herds of small animals, like tiny bison with circular horns and long shaggy hair. There was also a monster of sorts, an animal of bluish color about the size of a goat, but with a single horn protruding from the center of the forehead.

By this time, readers were lining up at newsstands waiting for the *Sun* to come off the press. But there was more to come, much more. Following a few more stories on lunar reindeer, horned bear and a variety of strange birds, Locke under a banner headline announced discovery of large winged creatures bearing a remarkable resemblance to humans. Herschel, according to Locke, assigned these creatures the Latin name vespertilio-homo, meaning flying men. They soared through the air like angels and alighted gracefully to stroll about in family groups. The Sun printed drawings to go with the story.

New Yorkers talked about nothing else but the discovery of life on the moon. Even the *New York Times* conceded that these scientific revelations were logical and reasonable. A ladies' club in Springfield collected funds to send missionaries to the moon. Day rubbed his hands as circulation soared.

Finally the two conspirators became worried. They had started something they could not stop. A way had to be found to terminate the hoax. Day left it up to Locke. In his final story — after telling how the flying families "spent their happy hours collecting various fruits in the woods" — the star reporter went on to tell of an unfortunate accident at the observatory. One night, he explained, after Herschel had completed his observations, a careless attendant left the telescope facing directly to the east. When the African sun arose next day, the heat burned a 15-foot hole in the delicate reflecting chamber. In a major tragedy for science, the marvelous telescope was utterly destroyed.

Somehow however, perhaps inevitably, the truth of the matter leaked out. In pious outrage every newspaper on the East Coast denounced the *Sun* for the monstrous deception. But the public didn't seem to care. The *Sun* continued to lead all New York papers in circulation long after relations between earth and moon had returned to normal. Leader of the attack against Day and the *Sun* was the formidable James Gordon Bennett of the rival *Herald*, but New Yorkers simply hooted at his indignation. There is nothing in the record to show whether star reporter Locke received a raise in pay.

In a Time of Crisis, the President Disappeared

At one point in the history of the United States, the President disappeared from sight, and the nation was without executive leadership for a week. This peculiar incident took place in the summer of 1893. Official Washington, including Congress, the cabinet, and the press, did not discover until much later that President Grover Cleveland had been confined for days aboard a vessel anchored in Long Island Sound.

Grover Cleveland was the only American President to serve two non-consecutive terms. When he took office for the second time in 1893, Cleveland found the country in a state of acute economic distress. Banks by the score were closing their doors, and savings institutions were refusing to release funds to depositors. Unemployment was widespread with reports of actual starvation in communities wholly dependent on industrial payrolls. Cleveland was convinced the trouble was the result of mismanagement by his Republican predecessor Benjamin Harrison and set out to correct the disastrous slide with a few corrective recommendations to Congress.

On June 15 the President asked the White House physician to look at a small sore spot on the roof of his mouth. Promptly the doctor sent an anonymous tissue sample to the Army Medical Museum, and just as promptly a report came back bearing the ominous word "malignant." Cleveland swore the doctor to secrecy, and even withheld the news from Vice President Adlai Stevenson.

A presidential illness at that particular time could only worsen the mood of pervasive pessimism then hovering like a cloud over the nation. Next, Cleveland sent a telegraph message to New York summoning an old fishing crony to the White House, Dr. Joseph Bryant, an eminent member of his profession. Presidential Adviser Daniel Lamont was admitted to the secret, and quietly the three men planned what had to be done.

On June 30 President Cleveland delivered to the Congress a message spelling out his recommendations for economic recovery. The program was extensive and ambitious, obviously planned with considerable care. That evening the President disappeared, and it was not until years later that the full story of his absence came to light.

In the early evening of that day, three men boarded a train from Washington to New York, traveling behind drawn curtains in a private compartment. No bodyguards were present since this responsibility had not yet been assigned to the Secret Service. In New York a public horse cab transported the trio to the waterfront, where a launch was waiting to ferry the party out to the steam yacht *Oneida* lying at anchor in the East River. Commodore Elias C. Benedict, owner of the luxurious craft, greeted his guests on arrival, and the vessel immediately moved down river in the darkness.

Next morning the *Oneida* was anchored in the glassy smooth waters of Long Island Sound. Below deck the main salon had been converted into a floating surgery with a team of doctors and nurses standing by to operate on the President. Because the patient weighed in excess of 300 pounds and suffered from high blood pressure, there was genuine reason for concern. Since the use of ether seemed too risky, the anesthesia applied was nitrous oxide, the new "laughing gas" then coming into favor among dentists.

The surgery itself took several hours, and when it was completed the patient was moved into a stateroom. Unfortunately, on the third day of recovery the doctors decided that additional tissue should be removed, and the procedure was repeated. At this point some of those present proposed that the whole attempt at secrecy be abandoned and the patient moved to a proper hospital in New York. But even in the best of circumstances such a move would unavoidably produce nationwide publicity with the nasty aroma of scandal. The President's friends prevailed over the opinions of the doctors.

Finally on July 5, the *Oneida* once more glided to shore and deposited the sick man at a dock near the Cleveland summer home in Massachusetts. Since the President was weak, in considerable pain, and unable to speak clearly, a bulletin was issued saying that he was suffering from rheumatism and would spend some time in the sunshine nursing this troublesome ailment. Three weeks later, Cleveland was back in Washington, ready to do battle on all fronts on the economic problems of the nation. His efforts earned for him a glittering reputation for honesty and for efficiency in removing cobwebs from a lethargic executive government.

Twenty-eight years later, at the age of 84, Dr. William Keen, the oral surgeon who actually operated on Cleveland, appeared again at an important moment in the illness of a prominent American. In August, 1921, while vacationing nearby, Dr. Keen was summoned to Campobello Island in New Brunswick as a consultant in diagnosing the illness of Franklin D. Roosevelt, tragically stricken with polio that summer.

U.S. President Banned Christmas Trees

President Theodore Roosevelt, who came to the White House in 1901, was a dedicated conservationist and was fanatically opposed to the display of Christmas trees in American homes or business establishments.

The redoubtable Teddy was convinced that because of the growing demand for evergreen trees America's forests would soon be stripped bare. Accordingly, although the Christmas tree had been an established White House tradition for more than 20 years at the time, the new President announced that there would be no more, and he urged every American to follow his example by putting an end to this wasteful practice.

Public reaction to the President's call for a ban on Christmas trees was less than completely enthusiastic. The President's own sister, whom the five Roosevelt children called Aunt Bannie, gave a great Christmas party for her nieces and nephews at her house in 1901. The children spent the day there with gifts arrayed under the tree.

On the following Christmas, 1902, the children had their own tree hidden in the closet of an upstairs bedroom. Inevitably, the President discovered it but did no more than deliver a lecture on conservation. But the ban against Christmas trees in the White House was adamantly maintained year after year.

In December 1906, a citizen in New York, feeling sorry for the White House children, sent them a Christmas tree and a box of ornaments. The gift was summarily returned with a brusque letter stating that the children of the President were not allowed to accept presents from people they did not know.

Although agricultural experts kept insisting that the only thing wrong with cutting Christmas trees was the lack of planning and management, national debate on the subject grew fierce. In a few years shortages of trees began to develop after dealers had cut down all the easy ones without regard for renewal of the forests.

Conservationists by this time were in full cry with a well-organized campaign to stop the commercial marketing of trees altogether. On the other hand, Gifford Pinchot, first great American exponent of scientific forestry, disagreed with all these restrictive plans, pointing out that Christmas trees could be cultivated and harvested like any other farm crop without damage to the ecology.

Nevertheless the President designated 150 million acres of public land as a national preserve upon which no trees could be cut.

In support of the national crusade, prominent women's magazines launched a campaign to abolish the Christmas tree by replacing it with an object called a Jacob's Ladder. This contraption consisted of an ordinary stepladder wrapped in cheesecloth and decorated with evergreens and candles

Illustrations depicted numerous imaginative possibilities for the thing, with presents arranged on the floor around the feet or displayed in order of size on the steps. Despite the backing of the foremost publishers catering to women and the home, the idea was not well received. As a national project, Jacob's Ladder was a disaster.

Another public relations campaign by newspapers and magazines advocated that only families with small children should be allowed to have Christmas trees. Like the idea of the stepladder, this brainstorm drew little response from the public.

Long after Theodore Roosevelt left the White House in 1909 the Christmas tree battle continued, while at the same time its popularity among American families expanded year after year. Shortages in supply became acute in the big eastern cities after a time, until by 1920 farmers bringing trees to market from Maine and Vermont had to be alert for hijackers.

A shotgun became standard equipment for the hardy souls bringing the spirit of Christmas to the cities.

With the passage of time, Pinchot's ideas on scientific forest management began to win acceptance. Farmers discovered that they could grow evergreen trees on scrub land that was good for little else, thus providing a new cash crop for a very small investment.

By 1930 Christmas tree farming was well established as a profitable business. One of the country's best-known and most successful cultivators about that time was another Roosevelt, a cousin of the original, irrepressible Teddy — Franklin D. Roosevelt of Hyde Park, New York.

As everyone knows this gentleman farmer had other interests besides trees, but his model plantation provided living testimony to the wisdom of the scientific principles preached for so long by Gifford Pinchot.

MISCELLANEOUS ESSAYS

for the
Back of the Book

Will 200-Year-Old Prophecy Come True?

(First Published 4 July 1975)

About two hundred years ago, when the American Colonies were fighting for independence, a British historian named Tyler published a gloomy prognosis for the future of democracy. "A democracy cannot exist," said Tyler, "as a permanent form of government. It can only exist until the voters discover that they can vote themselves largess from the public treasury. From that moment on, the majority always votes for the candidates promising the most benefits from the public treasury..." As a consequence, according to Tyler, the democratic system is bound to collapse because of loose fiscal policy, and will inevitably be followed by a dictatorship.

Today on the eve of the national bicentennial of democracy, many Americans are suffering from a form of visceral discomfort that no pharmaceutical remedy can reach. The ailment, affecting millions of citizens from coast to coast, is expressed by a gnawing sense of dismay caused by the spectacle of incredible disarray into which our national affairs have fallen. This dismay is compounded by bewilderment as Americans ask themselves: What has happened to our country? Why does misfortune face us from every direction?

Our economic system, once the wonder of the world, is in serious trouble, with a combination of depression and inflation contributing to unemployment and plummeting productivity. Neither the Congress nor the Executive Department can offer any solution, and some authorities predict a catastrophic worsening of the situation as energy supplies diminish. Crime continues to flourish, with enforcement agencies seemingly helpless to slow the proliferation. The educational system is faltering at all levels and is notably failing in the elementary task of providing functional education to new generations. In the meantime, our children are morally and literally going to pot. The debacle of Watergate and the shock waves continuing to radiate from the core depict a level of depravity in political leadership previously beyond the imagination of most

Americans. Not only are the most fundamental virtues flouted at will by people in high places, but the shabby selfish minds of some officials scoff at the presence of these virtues in others.

In the field of international relations, the picture of American stature is no brighter. Military, political, and diplomatic influence decline simultaneously. Prestige diminishes virtually from day to day, and our loss of dignity inspires audacious insult from petty sources. Consortia of opportunists — like the Barbary pirates of old — conspire to pick American pockets by fixing profiteer prices on such commodities as oil, coffee, sugar, and even bananas. Those pipsqueak nations that delight in using their votes to frustrate the United States in the General Assembly of the UN have too soon forgotten that they owe their existence and their political independence to the inspiration of American leadership in the world community. Many of our allies around the world now frankly place a price tag on their friendship. Such overt cynicism can only stem from contempt and from distrust of what we say and what we promise.

Add to the above the imminent threat of nationwide strikes, a bankrupt railroad system, uncontrollable traffic in drugs, plus a continuing subsurface rumble of possible racial violence, and America the Beautiful seems marred by an inordinate number of flaws.

Altogether, as it stands the vista cannot be regarded as encouraging, either at home or abroad. The American on Main Street is understandably puzzled. What has happened to everything? Where are the hallmarks of American greatness upon which our traditions are founded? Have the ideals of Adams, Madison, and Jefferson become old hat, to be discarded and abandoned forever? Can America no longer produce great minds and great public servants like John C. Calhoun, William Jennings Bryan, and Teddy Roosevelt? Or is the nation instead condemned to a pedestrian future characterized by mediocrity and regression?

Obviously there is justification for the pervasive sense of national dismay, but the time for despair is not yet with us. Even now in the nadir of our discontent, the quest for answers and solutions to national problems becomes more vigorous. And despite the pessimism of the fainthearted, answers are beginning to emerge.

Dismay, in a word, must never be confused with despair. The two are not the same.

It is yet too early to speak of a new enlightenment in America, but a fresh glimmer of hard, pragmatic understanding can be seen creeping over the horizon of tomorrow. The light is visible in the public pronouncements by leaders of business and industry and in some fresh new thinking coming out of the universities — not, notably, in the voices of political leadership in Washington. Critical self-analysis as a prerequisite for national reorientation is being initiated by corporation presidents and intellectuals outside of government. The findings of these analysts are far from complete; but, as a beginning, a degree of understanding is emerging to provide the basis for intelligent change.

Thus in the light of fuller understanding it can now be shown that the fiasco of our international relations over the past 30 years can be traced to the most fundamental and cardinal of all failings — Pride, the essential flaw that mars the character of all tragic heroes in literature.

The United States was thrust into the role of world leadership at the end of World War II, a young nation with but limited experience in the intricacies of global maneuver. We didn't know it at the time, but we were venturing into a game of adversary relationships in which the rules were made by the other players. But we proved to be an immediate success. The Atlantic Charter, formation of the United Nations, the Marshall Plan and the NATO alliance all combined to flood the American national ego with a dangerous overdose of adrenalin. Intoxicated by our success, we disdained any longer to recognise a limit on our capacity to influence events. As a result, our judgment in foreign affairs soon became tarnished by arrogance. The Ugly American, armed with greenbacks and propaganda, popped up around the world in the most unlikely places. Like single-minded missionaries of an earlier era we sought to clothe the heathen in ideas labeled "Made in USA." We were dedicated to the maintenance and support of "democracy" wherever it might be found, and not surprisingly that term was soon stripped of any real meaning.

Vietnam was only the most spectacular of our ill-starred overseas adventures. It was spectacular because of the heartless expenditure of human life, but in terms of wanton waste of treasure its $100 billion price tag has been matched by equally unproductive ventures elsewhere.

The $100 billion boondoggle has been easily surpassed in our bounty to India, a militaristic state we have sustained since it attained independence in 1947. A democracy in name only, India has been consistently opposed to United States policies. We have no cultural or ideological interests in common, yet when we wrote off India's food bill to the United States as a bad debt in 1960 it proved to be the largest financial transaction in the entire history of intergovernmental relations — bigger even than the reparations settlements following the first world war. Similarly, nobody even pretends any more that South Korea is now or ever was a democracy, and nobody knows for sure if any vestiges of democracy ever existed in Afghanistan. These two recipients of dollar diplomacy are simply more examples of our blind attempts to influence events by flooding the arena with money.

It is hardly surprising that these high-flying chickens have come home to roost and that 30 years of nonproductive economic activity have at last dealt a major blow to the domestic economic structure.

As for our difficulties here at home, some of the root causes are now being identified with more positive definition. One major factor is a loss of national perspective. We have lost sight of the meaning of democracy and of the functions and responsibilities of citizenship in a democratic society. Certainly, by definition, government machinery in a democracy is properly subservient to the people responsible for its creation. Yet here in the 1970s no one can deny that the American people are subservient to government. More than three million persons now work for the Federal Government and the national debt built up by proliferating bureaucracy has multiplied 300 times since 1900.

The basic definition of a citizen in a democracy states that a citizen is one who contributes to the general welfare. But this relationship has become twisted in our experience, and the number of citizens who do not contribute is growing dangerously. Apart from social security for older workers, government spending to subsidize general welfare, health, education, and public housing now amounts to $110 billion annually. This is the equivalent of financing a new Vietnam war every year.

But as we improve the capacity to identify our faults or shortcomings, what, realistically, are the chances of bringing about any improvement? The president of a chain of American insurance companies, speaking recently in Washington on the subject, estimates that the great American middle class — about 80 per cent of the population — is being stuck with an unfair share of the bills for our national mismanagement. It is this 80 per cent who are frustrated, angry, and suffering from the stomachache mentioned above. Collectively they possess the votes and the money necessary to impose their wishes on government. In 1976 they will reaffirm the true meaning of American Democracy and lead the way to a better society and a greater nation. Otherwise we may have to admit that the Englishman Tyler was right.

Women Seize Political Power

During the weeks following every national election, a process of analysis and evaluation takes place. In these dozens of studies, journalists, politicians, and college professors attempt to explain what happened at the polls and what can be expected to happen next time. One such study just released predicts that the next President or Vice President of the United States will be a woman.

This positive forecast by a respected Washington authority is based on statistical data on voter performance in November and examination of the changing status of women in politics over the past ten years or so. Women are on the move in the arena of public power, says the prophet, with vigor and purpose unmatched by their militant sisters in the earlier stages of the feminist movement.

In the election of 1986, three times as many women ran for office as in 1984. This number includes six for the U.S. Senate, 54 for the House, nine for governorships, 11 for lieutenant governorships, and an amazing 1,800 for state legislatures. Sixteen of these races were woman-versus woman contests. Although a few spectacular disappointments captured the headlines, the contest of 1986 is already recognized as a year of triumphant achievement for females in politics as a whole. Strategists of both major parties foresee even more women running in 1988, solid energetic people who can be expected to work their way up through the ranks to higher levels of service.

A significant indicator of the improved status of women in politics is the flood of money flowing into the hands of candidates. Although Paula Hawkins lost her Senate race for reasons that had nothing to do with gender, money was never her problem as supporters poured $3.5 million into the fund. Generous campaign funding was also a factor in the Senate victory of Barbara Mikulski of Maryland. Although her photogenic opponent Linda Chavez had the blessing of the White House, the successful candidate was in a position to employ massive artillery tactics in appealing to the voters. Professional fund raisers report that women are less coy than previously about asking supporters for money, and it is a natural law of politics that money attracts money.

Additionally, the analysts point out that the winners in 1986 are not beginners to politics or ornamental candidates. The victorious women running for federal and statewide office have an average of ten years' experience in the public arena. A spokesperson for the nonpartisan National Women's Political Caucus observes that, "These women are high-caliber candidates, and they have earned the right to be in these races." Many have served for years in lesser offices. In Connecticut, Julie Belaga served five terms in the state legislature before deciding to run for governor, and Kay Orr of Nebraska had been state treasurer since 1981 before making her move for the statehouse.

Although not every woman was a winner, party leadership sent fewer "sacrificial lambs" into the battle than ever before. Every female nominated was a viable candidate with better than reasonable odds for victory. By contrast, many female candidates in 1984 were selected as political window dressing without a ghost of a chance. Understandably, most of these were slaughtered at the polls.

Experts now tend to agree that 1986 has been a "coming of age" for women in politics. Candidates no longer carry the burden of having to defend their femininity. Like their male competitors, the ladies can run on their qualifications as political leaders and credible applicants for larger responsibilities. A significant factor also noted in 1986 is that female candidates no longer stress "women's issues" to the exclusion of other voter interests having equal or greater importance. Democratic hopeful Harriet Woods of Missouri raised $3.5 million for her Senate bid but based her campaign on the single issue of abortion. She lost.

Apart from the question of who won and who lost, the election of 1986 has proved to be a turning point for American women and for female leaders in particular. Everywhere the numbers are up as more females run for office, more women manage campaigns, and more people of both sexes donate money. While the post-game analysis continues, both major parties are joyful and optimistic about what they see for the future. Republicans are convinced that the GOP inventory of high-profile, talented, and experienced women is richer and deeper than the Democratic collection, particularly at the higher levels of public service. Democrats, on the other hand undismayed by the Ferraro experiment of 1980, are certain that the party can move upward to new heights by exploiting the electrifying impact of petticoat politics.

Of course all the old arguments remain unanswered. Advocates of feminist leadership maintain that women have a sharper perception of ethical and moral values; they are the principal custodians of humane civilizing instincts and have a natural esteem for stability in community life with prospects for a peaceful future. The masculine view is that all political action is essentially based on application of force in varying degrees, a task better suited to the natural capacities of the male.

In any event, no immediate reason can be found to believe that the male politician has become an endangered species in 1986.

Great Depression Legacy Remains (1979)

During the past week the stock market took a severe beating as interest rates in the banking community climbed another notch or two, reaching incredibly new highs. Simultaneously on international markets the dollar and other paper currencies continued to suffer in their losing battle against gold. Among the people who are supposed to know about such things, predictions of a moderate economic slump, measurable in months, began to take on a more ominous note. Prophecies of a global recession of unknowable intensity and duration were heard as the business week neared an end. The nation's press in the meantime took pains to remind readers that October of this year marks the 50th anniversary of the stock market crash of 1929, the opening scene in the dismal drama of the Great Depression.

There are those who maintain that such a thing can never happen again; a whole barricade of safeguards has been erected in the years since the great catastrophe happened. For one thing, Wall Street is no longer the epicenter of world finance as it once was. Today the money business is much more diversified and is stringently regulated by an elaborate system of controls, governmental and otherwise. No doubt a comparable disaster cannot befall again in precisely the same way, but in the spring of 1929, millions of Americans, including men of sound judgment, were supremely confident that the merry-go-round would go on whirling forever. In the summer of '29 the Dow stock average was hovering about 400. Who could imagine that after the bubble burst it would sink to an unbelievable 36 by 1922?

Oddly enough, there is no agreement as to what precise day the historic crash took place. Thus, Thursday, October 24, the first day upon which panic seized the market, has been regularly cited as the Black Thursday of the collapse. But professionals have always leaned to the following Monday or Tuesday, when the losses were far greater and when the volume of trading reached its all time high. Even the biographers of President Herbert Hoover have been unable to settle on any one day.

The most significant and enduring consequence of the stock market crash and the Great Depression which followed is the transformation effected in the role of the national government. President Herbert Hoover, who wrestled with the dragon throughout his term, adhered staunchly to principle and rejected the thought of any departure from what he regarded as traditional government propriety. When the Hoover administration assumed office in March 1929, the new president came to power under most auspicious circumstances. With a comfortable Republican majority in Congress, Hoover regarded the role of government as something like that of a benevolent chamber of commerce. However, by mid-summer the signs of emerging economic distress were unmistakable, and by the end of the term wheat was down from $1 a bushel to 38 cents; cotton was 6 cents a pound, and more than 12 million men were out of work.

By 1933, with the nation in the pit of despair and the unemployment rate at 25 percent, America welcomed the dictatorial policies of President Franklin Roosevelt when he assumed power as general manager of every aspect of the national destiny. With little or no hope in sight, the country was ready to accept any kind of radical innovation, and FDR obliged with a theatrical flourish. Two days after inauguration he closed all banks, and soon thereafter launched a massive program of public work projects, including CWA, WPA, CCC and NRA, among others. He paid farmers not to farm and tinkered with the money supply in exploratory experiments. When the Supreme Court dared to veto some of his measures, the energetic FDR set out to restructure the court to his liking. Other New Deal innovations included the Social Security program, now under fire from a number of sources, and home relief, which has developed into a frankenstein monstrosity.

In fairness let it be said that New Deal programs at the time contributed to the temporary alleviation of hunger and privation, but the fallacy behind New Deal philosophy was the assumption that economic manipulation and social engineering have a place as proper functions of government. Despite all the effort and ingenuity involved, the ambitious plans of Roosevelt's high-powered idealists did not work. By 1938, after five years of experimentation, the New Deal was largely discredited. In the election of that year Republicans swept in droves into the House and Senate, while picking up 13 governorships. This new Congress of 1939 arose in rebellion against the White House, slashing relief appropriations, killing presidential appointments, undoing tax policies, and dismantling some of the New Deal agencies. Six years after its audacious beginning, the New Deal had run aground.

Ironically, the New Deal was rescued from failure by the approach of war clouds in Europe and Asia, a process which proceeded by regular stages beginning about 1936. Factories began once again to hum, not in response to the artificial stimulus of government programs, but to meet the mounting demands for arms and ammunition in Europe. World War II followed quickly, and the mythology of the New Deal became caught up in the unprecedented national effort that went into winning the war decisively and dramatically. Out of all this grew the rationale, the justification, for the present role of government as manager, as master rather than servant of the people. This was the beginning of the belief, now an article of faith in American government, that all problems can be solved by inundating them with massive applications of money.

Several times since then the fatal flaws of this doctrine have been demonstrated. The Great Society programs of Lyndon Johnson were founded on the same heresy as the New Deal of 30 years earlier, and their failure has been only a little less spectacular. Crowning evidence of the ineffectiveness of government management of the civilian economy is seen in the inglorious chapter of history surrounding the war in Vietnam. Looking this week at the troubled state of the economy and the uncertain prospects for the months ahead, it seems clear that government policy must share a large measure of blame for the national predicament.

Seasonal Signs Point to Romance Ahead

An old romantic legend of the Christmas season tells the story of how Saint Nicholas saved the three daughters of a poor farmer from becoming old maids by giving each one a generous gift of money for her dowry.

In the darkness of night on December 6, feast day of Saint Nicholas, the mystical old gentleman crept quietly to the tumble-down cottage in the forest and dropped three bags of gold down the chimney. As a result each of the young maids was surrounded by numbers of serious admirers during the festive days of the holiday season.

This happy incident is memorialized even today by the three gold balls hanging over the door of a pawnbroker's shop, symbols of three bags of gold and a convenient source of ready money for the needy.

According to another romantic tradition of the season, unattached young girls can foresee certain glimpses of their forthcoming courtship and marriage by observing prescribed rituals handed down from earlier times. For example, on the feast day of Saint Barbara, which falls on December 4, the hopeful young lady should stand barefoot at dusk under a plum tree or a cherry tree and listen intently for a dog to bark. When the bark at last is heard, the sound will indicate the direction from which her future sweetheart will enter into her life.

On the same evening the girl must break a branch from the plum tree or cherry tree and place it indoors in a container of warm water near the fire. If the twig sprouts by Christmas Day, a joyous marriage can be expected early in the new year.

If the daughter of the house dutifully carries out her share of the kitchen chores in the days leading up to Christmas, further signs can provide information of importance. The skin of an apple, carefully pared off in a single unbroken spiral and then tossed in the fire, will assume the shape of the unknown suitor's initial before being consumed by the flames. Eggwhite scraped from the sides of the mixing bowl and dropped in a shallow pan of hot water will reveal a good likeness of the young man's profile.

On December 21 comes the feast of Saint Thomas, a very important day in the sequence of Christmas events. Bible students will remember that Thomas was the apostle who doubted, who refused to believe what was told by his associates unless a sign could be shown to him.

Accordingly, any portents or revelations encountered on this day are supposed to carry a special significance.

This day, the 21st, also marks the winter solstice, the point from which the sun begins the long journey back from darkness to bring renewed life and the promise of spring. Since this is also the longest night of the year, it was customary in olden times to pass away a part of the long darkness in dancing.

The girl who could dance until she was dizzy, and who then went to bed with her feet on the pillow and her head at the foot of the bed, was sure to dream of her future sweetheart through the rest of the darkness till dawn.

The feast of Saint Stephen, on the day after Christmas, is traditionally special for horses and horsemen. To insure her good fortune in affairs of the heart during the coming year, a young girl should fill her pocket with sugar lumps and pay a visit to residents of the stable.

If all the signs and signals should prove too confusing or contradictory, the system of olden days provided a final opportunity to clarify questions. The ritual of upsidedown sleeping repeated on the Eve of Saint Agnes, January 20, would resolve all doubts by insuring dreams that were dependable and informative.

But times change and old customs disappear as memories fade. Today's young people in search of signs and portents are more likely to consult a computer than the colorful oddities of nature. Nevertheless the spirit of hope and sentimentality is immutable.

How I Stopped the Show at St. Philomena's

When I was a boy in Ireland, age about eleven or twelve, Dada and Mama decided that I was unmanageable.

Their decision had something to do with an old clock that had stood from time immemorial, silent and useless, on the mantlepiece in our back parlor. Not only had it never worked in my lifetime, but indeed it may never have worked for a hundred years. One of the twin dials was supposed to show the phases of the moon, among other things, as illustrated by drawings of celestial objects like comets and stars.

One rainy afternoon I took the thing apart with my little screwdriver, arranging the assortment of springs, sprockets, and flywheels in display on the hearthrug before the fire. Here they lay when Dada and Mama returned from their absence. Within the week I was on a train bound for Saint Philomena's Convent School for Boys.

Saint Philomena's was in reality an isolated old country house surrounded by lawns and flower beds and identified only by a modest sign over the gatekeeper's cottage. A long outbuilding, formerly stables and carriage house, had been converted into a dormitory for about forty boys. Everything else took place at the big house which stood on a low hill overlooking the landscape.

The institution was operated by the Sisters of Faith and Hope, an austere order of nuns noted for their piety, learning, and discipline. Indeed, discipline was very much the strong point at Saint Philomena's. Anyone who thinks that physical restraint and corporal punishment are essential elements of discipline has never lived under the silken soft-sell of nun power. Conversation in the dining room was subdued; contact between cutlery and chinaware was noiseless, and the scrape of a chair leg against the oaken floor was almost a mortal sin. At the conclusion of each meal we sat with hands folded until the Sister in charge gave the signal to rise simultaneously. For school work we studied literature and Latin, among other things, but particularly drama. Notably and emphatically drama, for therein lies a tale.

Every spring, the school year at Saint Philomena's reached a resounding festive conclusion with presentation of an ambitious theatrical production for the edification of parents and the many friends of the institution. The annual event was a major navigation point in the history and tradition of the Sisters of Faith and Hope, the hallmark of communal achievement, and a symbol of dedication to culture.

Everybody participated in one way or another, each according to his or her talents. Kitchen workers and gardeners hammered sets together or painted scenery. A special team of nuns spent weeks designing and fitting costumes, while actors and their coaches slaved through countless hours of diligent rehearsal.

During my year in residence, the play chosen for spring presentation was Shakespeare's *The Merchant of Venice*, easily the best item in the bard's portfolio. Frankly I must confess to a feeling of smug satisfaction when Mother Superior announced the assignment of parts. No doubt because of my good looks I was chosen to be Bassanio.

Now Bassanio is not exactly the lead character in the play, but his problem constitutes the core of the plot. The romantic Bassanio, a gentleman of Venice, wishes to court the rich and beautiful widow Portia but lacks the money to do so properly. His good friend Antonio promises to help, but in doing so Antonio gets himself in trouble with Shylock, the friendly local moneylender.

Through a long procession of afternoons we practiced our parts in the Great Hall, which once a year was transformed into a theatre for the occasion. On the sidelines, with scripts in hand, exacting nuns monitored every syllable, every gesture, every motion of head or eyes.

Costumes at Saint Philomena's were something special, absolutely authentic and a work of art in each case. None of your usual whip, pin, and baste would do for the good sisters assigned to the task of needlework. As a gentleman of Venice I was fitted out with kidskin slippers ornamented with a silver buckle, thigh-high hose of burnished silk, and bloused breeches of soft green velvet. My shirt was ruffled, trimmed with lace at cuffs and collar, while a

Cavalier hat with pheasant plume completed the picture of a true Venetian dandy.

Came at last the great day, the culmination of collective effort by staff and students of Saint Philomena's. As the play opens, Bassanio makes his appearance about two minutes into the first act, following an exchange between Antonio and two secondary characters in which they set the scene for the story.

Peeking out from the wings while awaiting my cue, I could spy Dada and Mama seated among forty sets of happy parents in the foreground of the Great Hall. To one side I caught a glimpse of the bishop in rapt conversation with Mother Superior who managed somehow to look complacent and triumphant simultaneously. The rest of the nuns were arranged in smiling rows behind the parents and distinguished friends of the school.

Beside me in the wings stood Sister Jean Baptiste, with eyes glued to the action taking place on stage. As Antonio speaks his farewell to Salarino, she places a hand on my arm. This is my cue. At the moment the world came to an end.

Bassanio wet his pants.

No Lumps, No Burns, No Skin

When I was a boy in Ireland, the standard breakfast for the entire Irish population consisted of oatmeal porridge, better known among the common people as "stirabout." As a national institution, this lukewarm, sticky mush was dutifully ingested by everyone, the sinners and the saved, patrician and peasant, male and female alike. Some people added a bit of milk, or even cream in the upper circles of society. Epicures occasionally used substantial helpings of brown sugar, stirring it thoroughly into the pale potato-colored mass. Like or dislike had nothing to do with it; everybody in Ireland ate porridge as a simple habit of life—like saying prayers at bedtime or taking a bath on Saturday night.

Of course the world was much simpler and saner in those early days. Oatmeal in the raw was a straightforward grain commodity without any of the refinements or additives that clutter up contemporary subsistence. Quick-cooking oats or instant cereal had not yet been invented or thought of. Thus the daily process of preparing the family porridge was a lengthy undertaking involving considerable time, talent, and effort.

The kitchen at our home was a cavernous sunken chamber at the back of the house into which children were never admitted. Of course we peeked frequently through the tinted window leading off from the back parlor or lurked in the hall when adult traffic was moving back and forth.

Presiding over this mysterious region with its earthern floor and scary dark corners was a giant shadowy female known, when her name was mentioned at all, as Mrs. Brady (Dada called her Mrs. Coaldust, but even he never ventured to invade her kitchen). She made a lot of noise in the management of her domain, banging great iron pots on the stovetop and shoveling quantities of coal into the fire. She was unquestionably monarch of her special dark world and dictator of the family diet. Eileen, who had positive views about many things, once suggested that Mrs. Brady was actually a witch, and since Eileen was the eldest, the rest of us usually accepted her pronouncements as gospel.

Of necessity in the circumstances, our contact with Mrs. Brady was filtered through the person of Cassie. As part nursemaid and general family factotum, Cassie enjoyed unlimited right of passage between the world at the back of the house and the family rooms in front. As a matter of fact, Cassie was our liaison with the adult world in general, in good times and bad, for better or for worse. Thus we are indebted to Cassie for much of the information surrounding the memory of porridge for breakfast.

Every night, when the affairs of the day were finished, Mrs. Brady in her kitchen set about the task of preparing the porridge for family breakfast the following morning. In a large heavy pot she placed two simple ingredients, oatmeal and water, then stirred the two together with a long wooden paddle until the mixture reached boiling point. (Hence the term: "stirabout.")

Next, as the brew bubbled briskly, Mrs. Brady killed the fire by pulling a lever that dropped the hot coals into the ash receptacle. For some hours thereafter, the oatmeal continued to cook as the stove cooled through the evening. But strange things began to happen after Mrs. Brady had turned off the gaslights and disappeared into the night. For one thing, the porridge all too frequently stuck to the bottom of the pot and became scorched, a condition that served to permeate the porridge with a distinctive flavor and aroma.

Simultaneously, during the darkness, small doughy balls, like tumors, formed in the center of the mass. In size these might vary from the dimension of jellybeans to the magnitude of golf balls. Finally, as the heat of the kitchen was replaced by cool night air, a thick crust like pigskin or plastic formed on the top surface of the mixture.

Sometime before dawn next morning, Mrs. Brady reappeared in her kitchen, stoked up her fire, and once more stirring briskly, brought the porridge to a fresh boil. In the process of course, the tumors, the scorched fragments, and morsels of pigskin were nicely distributed uniformly throughout.

In those growing-up years, we children—all five of us—slept in a big bed on the top floor, right under the attic. The two littlest ones, because their legs were shorter, slept at the bottom. Since the routines of bedtime and getting up in the morning were conducted under the direction of Cassie, the arrangement involved no more than nominal bickering. But we were invariably noisy in the early mornings after Cassie pulled the curtains and announced time for breakfast. Even as we scrambled for socks and stuff, the chant began, spontaneously and unvarying in content. "No Lumps, No Burns, No Skins."

Down the stairs we skipped, a five-part tangle of chattering energy with a single theme. At the first landing, we tip-toed over the thick carpet outside the double oak door behind which Mama and Dada still slept in wait for a more respectable hour to arise. When we reached the door of the back parlor, our chant was again in crescendo: No Lumps, No Burns, No Skins.

At the end of the table sat Cassie behind a great tureen of porridge, ladle in hand, five bowls conveniently ready. As we took our places the chant faded, and each one cautiously, hopefully, and vainly stirred the concoction of breakfast nourishment. Lumps! Burns! Skins! In some respects, Cassie was a stern disciplinarian and withheld the servings of hot cocoa until the last sticky morsel of stirabout had disappeared.

With the inevitable passage of time, that nest in due course became empty, and eventually disappeared, having served its purpose in the endless dialectic of human experience. Vivid memories remain, blessed memories endowed with the magic of perpetual endurance. Among them is Oatmeal Porridge and the war cry of childhood: No Lumps, No Burns, No Skins.

Tenderfoot Dream
First Published at Fairbanks, Alaska, 1952

The other midnight I tossed and turned,
After eating a steak that was slightly burned,
After drinking a flagon or more of wine,
I was paying the price of a weakness of mine.
    My Ulcers.
But presently I dozed and dreamed,
And in the dream, to me it seemed,
I floated gently over town,
In a pair of wings and a flowing gown.
    Deceased.
I gazed on the pleasant scene below,
Fairbanks tucked in a vale of snow.
The neon lights of the "First-Last Chance,"
I sighed and gave a second glance.
    Wuz Thirsty
Another ghost on a cloud nearby,
Came drifting close—an older guy.
An old sourdough with a dingy beard,
He looked at the town below and sneered.
    Disdainful.
"Look at those softies living there.
With their plush-lined bars and neon glare.
Such decadence, if you're asking me,
Is not what life's supposed to be."
    Scornful.
We fluttered down from our cloudy seat,
Landed heel and toe on Cushman Street,
"Come on," says he, "let's look around,
I'll tell you just what ails the town."
    A Critic.
"Cocktail bars and Stateside steak,
Monuments for the stomach's sake,
Fancy grub from the seven seas,
He-men don't need such foods as these.

   They're Sissy."
"In the good old days, when men were men,
We had no fancy cafes then.
Whiskey straight and simple grub,
And better men we were then, Bub."
   He meant it.
In time this windy Dan McGrew,
Tired me out, as bores will do,
I tapped him gently on the wing,
"Let's talk of something else, old thing."
   But did he?
"I first came here in Nineteen-Three,
Where the Nordale stands there stood a tree.
I stopped the dogs and turned them loose,
While I thawed a piece of frozen moose.
   Good Eating."
"All winter long in the bitter cold,
I followed the endless search for gold.
When food got low and things looked bad,
I shrugged and managed with what I had.
   'Twas rugged."
"Caribou soup and rabbit stew,
For me and fourteen huskies too,
Found our grub in nature's way.
Had a leg of wolf on Christmas Day.
   Bit gamey."
"Hunger and cold were the common lot,
One by one my dogs were shot.
Hungry man finds food that suits,
On New Year's Day I ate my boots."
   Note below*
"In arctic cold I fought with fate,
Without complaint on what I ate,
Came in time the first of May,
I lay me down and passed away.
   From Ulcers."
*Local legend says it can be done. We don't believe it.

From a Lady to her New Daughter-in-Law

A Blessing

Once, in another time, he and I were one,
One in flesh and blood and in the mystical spirit that is life,
And joined inseparably forever by the love that flowers
From the wonder of creation.

Hand in hand, together we explored the meandering pathways of awakening years,
Conquering small dragons along the way, finding fresh delight in every new discovery,
While gathering bouquets of memories from the garden of childhood,
And wrapped in the happiness that derives from heartbeats in harmony.

With pride and gladness I now commend him to your keeping.
He comes to you clothed in a legacy of steadfast, enduring values.
The fabric woven by upright, earnest Christian forebears,
The garment fitted to his shoulders with fond parental care.

As you now rejoice in his manhood, I wish you fulfillment, good fortune and tranquil years.
Above all, remember in your heart, your life and mine have been jointly blessed forever,
As we share God's love in an everlasting miracle — the immortality of the human spirit.

30 April 1994

Christmas Alone

The Laughter of Children—the whisper of snow
The dolls in the toyshops, row upon row,
All over town does the magic appear,
Once more it's December, and Christmas is near,
There's turkey and tinsel, and wondering stares,
As the children gaze wide-eyed at fabulous wares.
There are smiles on the faces of folks passing by,
With mysterious bundles piled ever so high.
But it's hard for the man who's alone on the streets,
To share in the joy of the people he meets.
There's a lump in his throat, in his heart there's a stone,
As he faces the prospect of Christmas alone,
He envies the parents—he envies their smiles,
And his mind leaps away for thousands of miles—
To a very small girl in a faraway place,
And his eyes wrinkle up as he pictures her face,
As she places her packages under the tree,
"There's a present for Daddy from Mommy and me,"
The soldier looks up at the faraway skies,
And the hurt in his soul could be seen in his eyes.
His lips make a whisper that no one could hear,
"Merry Christmas, my lovely, Merry Christmas, my dear!"
But Christmas withal is the season for prayer,
For hope and fulfillment and surcease from care,
May God hear the whispers of all who must roam,
For peace and goodwill and next Christmas at home.

Index

Adams, Abigail Smith 6, 126
Adams, John 6, 126
Adolphus, King Gustavus 103
Alexander I, Czar 130
"Alkali Ike" 137
Allen, Florence Ellinwood 87
American democracy 179
Anthony, Susan B. 95, 125, 128
Arguello, Dona Concepcion 130
Arnold, Gen. Henry H. "Hap" 152
Bactrian camels 162
Baldwin, Faith 37
Barry, Dr. James 19
Bassanio 193
Beale, Lt. Edward 162
Belaga, Julie 185
Benedict, Commodore Elias C. 172
Bennett, James Gordon 170
Black Bart 153
Blaine, James G. 95
Bloomer, Amelia 128
Bly, Nellie 36, 38
Bolton, C. E. 154
Bonny, Anne 92
Boot, Joe 99
Bouvier, Marie 78
Boz Ball 167
Bradford, Andrew 35
"Bread Lady of New Orleans" 81
Bridget of Ireland 108
Brinville, Celeste 110
Bryant, Dr. Joseph 171
Butler, Benjamin 95
Butterick, Ebenezer 83
Calhoun, John C. 14, 16
Calvin, John 61
Cardis, Luis 149
Cashman, Peggy 31
"Casket Girls" 132
Catherine I 113
Catt, Carrie Chapman 125, 128
Cavanagh, Kit 119
Charles, King 123
Chauncey, Charles 123
Chavez, Linda 184
Chlorus, Emperor 52
Christina, Queen 103
Christmas Day 190
Claflin, Tennessee 28
Cleveland, Frances Folsom 41
Cleveland, Grover 41, 95, 171
Cody, Buffalo Bill 148
Cole, King 52
Columbus, Christopher 121
"Company of Saint Patrick" 145
Constantine 52
Corday, Charlotte 85
Dahomey, women's army of 119
Dana, Maj. Gen. N. T. 158
Das Kapital 165
Davis, Sen. Jefferson 162
Day, Benjamin 169
Demorest, Madame 82
Demorest, Nell Curtis 82
Demorest, Will 82
Dickens, Charles 167
Dickens, Kate 167
Dix, Dorothea 89
Donelson, Emily 11
dromedaries 162

Duke de Guise 62
Duke of Ferrara 61
Eaton, John Henry 10
Eaton, Peggy O'Neale 10
Edmonds, Sarah 21
Eliot, T.S. 37
Emerson, Ralph Waldo 36
Endicott, John 123
Ervin, Evander M. 143
Eve of Saint Agnes 191
feast day of Saint Barbara 190
feast day of Saint Nicholas 190
feast of Saint Stephen 191
feast of Saint Thomas 191
Ferraro, Geraldine 186
Fillmore, Millard 162
Fisher, Mary 63
Fisher, William 148
Franklin, Ann 35
Franklin, Benjamin 3
Frost, Robert 37
Fry, Elizabeth 70
Fuller, Margaret 36, 101
Gardiner, David 160
Gardiner, Julia 160
Garfield, James 67
Gilmer, Thomas W. 160
Goddard, Mary Katherine 3
Goddard, Samuel 3
Goddard, William 3
Goffe, Frances 124
Goffe, William 123
Grant, Julia 24, 26
Grant, Nellie 26
Grant, Ulysses S. 24, 26, 29
"the Great Depression" 187
Greeley, Horace 29, 36, 102, 164

Greenhow, Rose 16
Hale, Sarah Josepha 36
Harding, Warren 73
Harrison, Benjamin 171
Hart, Pearl 99
Haughery, Margaret 80
Hayes, Lucy 33, 72
Hayes, Rutherford B. 33
Helena 52
Herschel, Sir John 169
Hodges, Bill 153
Hoover, Herbert 187
Howard, Judge Charles H. 149
Hubbard, Governor of Texas 150
Hurst, Fanny 37
Jackson, Andrew 10, 13
"a Jacob's Ladder" 175
Jefferson, Thomas 7, 8, 130
Jones, John Paul 138
Jones, Mary Harris "Mother" 49
June, Jeannie 83
Justinian, Emperor 105
Keen, Dr. William 173
Keil, William 140
Kelly, Lizzie 35, 38
Kempe, Margery 55
Kennon, Beverly 160
Kingsley, Mary 57
Lamont, Daniel 171
La Navidad 122
Lee, Charles 134
Lee, Robert E. 25
Leslie, Frank 66
Leslie, Miriam Follin Squier 66
Lincoln, Abraham 21, 25, 157
Lincoln, Mary Todd 24
Locke, Richard 169

Lockwood, Belva Ann 94
Lowe, Juliette "Daisy" Gordon 45
Lowe, William 46
Lowell, Amy 37
"Lydia Pinkham's Vegetable Compound" 98
Madison, Dolley 8, 41, 160
Madison, James 8
Marat, Jean Paul 85
Marx, Karl 164
Mather, Increase 124
Maxcey, Virgil 160
The Merchant of Venice 193
Mikulski, Barbara 184
Mills, Ann 119
Monroe, Harriet 37
Morris, Esther 68
Mott, Lucretia 127
Napoleon, Emperor 142
New York Herald 170
New York Sun 169
New York Times 170
New York Tribune 164
Ney, Marshal Michel 142
Ney, Peter Stuart 143
Nightingale, Florence 20
oatmeal porridge 195
Oneida 172
"the Oregon" 159
Orr, Kay 185
Pankhurst, Emmaline 125
Parker, Dorothy 37
Paul, Alice 125, 128
Pauline Carroll 158
"the Peacemaker" 159
Peter the Great 114
Pinchot, Gifford 174

Pinkerton, Alan 17
Pinkham, Lydia Estes 97
Pinkham, Isaac 97
Pony Express 147
Porter, Horace 138
Pound, Ezra 37
Pry, Paul 35
Rackman, Danny 92
Reed, James 74
Renee of France 61
Rezanov, Baron Nikolai 130
Riley, John 145
Rind, Clementina 35
Rogers, Benjamin 143
Rogers, Robert 143
Roosevelt, Alice 43
Roosevelt, Edith 43
Roosevelt, Franklin D. 88, 173, 175, 188
Roosevelt, Theodore 43, 72, 174
Royal, Anne 35
Russell, John 123
Russell, Majors, and Wadell 147
Russian Battalion of Death 120
Saint Nicholas 190
Saint Patrick 109
Saint Philomena's Convent School for Boys 192
Sanger, Margaret 76
Santa Anna, General 146
Schurz, Carl 33
Scott, Winfield 146
Shaw, Anna Howard 128
Shirley, Myra Belle 74
Silver, John 151
Singer, Isaac 82
Sousa, John Philip 41

Squier, Ephriam 66
Stanton, Elizabeth Cady 125, 127
Stanton, Harriot 125
Stanton, Secretary of War, 25
Starr, Belle 75
Starr, Sam 75
Stephens, Ann S. 36
Stevenson, Adlai 171
"stirabout" 195
Stockton, Capt. Robert F. 159
Stone, Lucy 128
Strauss, Levi 136
Stuart, Miranda 19
Sultan of Turkey 64
Sultana 157
Taft, Nellie Herron 72
Taft, William Howard 72
Tate, Billy 147
Taylor, Zachary 145
Theodora, Empress 105
Thompson, Dorothy 37
Thompson, Frank 21
Thompson, Sarah Edmonds 23
Timothy, Elizabeth 35
Turkish riflewomen 120
Tyler, British historian 179
Tyler, John 13, 160
Tyler, Julia 13
Universal Friend 59
Upshur, Abel P. 160
U.S.S. Princeton 159
VanBuren, Martin 10
Victoria, Queen 45
Walker, William 155
Washington, George 4, 134
Waterman, Bob 40
Webster, Daniel 164

Whalley, Edward 123
"Wild Rose of the Confederacy" 16
Wilkinson, Jemina 59
Wilson, Edith Bolling Galt 47
Wilson, Woodrow 47
Woodhull, Victoria Claflin 28, 128
Woods, Harriet 185
Zenger, Catherine 35

Bibliography

Turner, Orsamur, *History of the Pioneer Settlement of Phelps and Gorham's Purchase and Moore's Reserve* (1851) pp 153-62

The New Yorker, May 19, 1936

Hudson, David, *History of Jemima Wilkinson* (1829)

Webster's New World Dictionary of the American Language (The World Publishing Company, Cleveland and New York 1959)

Webster's New World Dictionary, Encyclopedic Edition (The World Publishing Company 1959)

Willard, Frances E and Livermore, Mary E., *A Woman of the Century* (1893).

Who's Who in America, 1916-17

Literary Digest, June 16, 1917

The Woman Citizen, June 2, 1917

The Suffragist, Mary 26, 1917

Case and Comment, August 1917

The Evening Star (Washington), May 19, 1917

New York Times, May 20, 1917